BENEATH A ROUGHER SEA

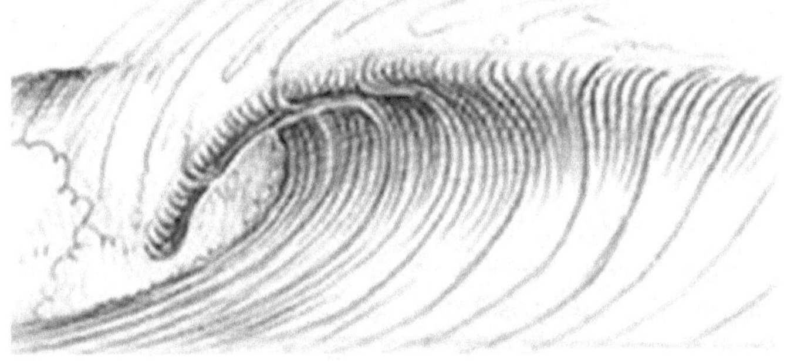

SUSMITA BAGCHI

ISBN 978-93-52016-23-5
© Susmita Bagchi 2016

Cover: Riyaz Merchant, Kitsuné India
Layouts: Chandravadan Shiroorkar, Leadstart Design
Printing: Thompson Press

First Published in India 2016 by
JUFIC BOOKS
An imprint of LEADSTART PUBLISHING PVT LTD
Unit 25/26, Building A/1
Near Wadala RTO, Wadala (East), Mumbai 400037,
INDIA
T + 91 22 24046887 + 91 96 99933000 F +91 22 40700800
E info@leadstartcorp.com W www.leadstartcorp.com

TO SUBROTO

ABOUT THE AUTHOR

SUSMITA BAGCHI has published eight novels, seven short-story collections and a travelogue, all in Odia. Her work has been translated into English, Hindi, Marathi, Telugu, Kannada and Malayalam. Among her many awards are the Odisha Sahitya Akademi award and the Utkal Samman. She lives in Bangalore with her husband Subroto. They have two daughters, Neha and Niti.

AUTHOR'S NOTE

The idea of a novel on mental health first came to me about twelve years ago. Uncertain whether I could do the subject justice, I hesitated and let it go. But the subject kept returning to my mind. Finally, in 2010, I decided to talk to a psychiatrist friend, Dr Vivek Benegal, Professor of Psychiatry at the National Institute of Mental Health and Neuro Sciences (NIMHANS). He thought it was a great idea, given the widespread ignorance on the subject. Over the next few days he spent many hours telling me more about it. That was the turning point. Vivek, just a 'thank you' is not enough: I owe you a great deal.

After my conversations with Vivek, I started my research. People in my family and some among my friends have experienced mental illness. But in the course of my research, I discovered that most families have instances of mental illness in their immediate or extended circle. These are sometimes undiscovered, or glossed over, or pushed aside in denial. The ignorance on the issue of mental health is pervasive. Learning this made me even more determined to write this novel.

Once a rough draft was ready, I reached out to Shrutkeerti Khurana, a freelance editor. She helped me make the narrative flow better, encouraging and supporting me over the course of many rounds of revisions. She was a delight to work with. Thank you, Shrutee.

Mental health is a complex subject. Hoping to catch any scientific errors, I decided to run my manuscript past another psychiatrist friend, Dr Prabha Chandra, who is also a Professor at NIMHANS. Prabha went through the entire work in great detail; she was very helpful in pointing out issues with both the use of certain medical terms as well as with the depiction of a few situations in the story. I am indebted to her.

My husband, Subroto, was taken with the idea right from the beginning. He listened to my stories, watched my progress, and soothed the frustrations I felt along my journey. He did not let me give up when internal and external factors threatened to make me do so. I don't think this book would have seen the light of day without him.

Our daughters, Neha and Niti, are delighted that finally I have written a book in a language that they can read. All my books have so far been originally written in Odia, my mother tongue. While writing the novel, I often reached out to Neha and Niti for their comments. Their love for their mother notwithstanding, both of them were objective and frank in their encouragement and their critique. It was Niti who thought of Cowper's poem and picked out the name for this novel. It really helps to have English and Classics majors in the family.

My parents, Sakuntala and Harihar Panda, apart from being writers themselves, are the most doting parents one could have. Their 'Yes, you can' attitude has always emboldened me to explore new subjects. They take immense pride in my writing and I am grateful for that.

Once my final draft was ready, I reached out to Swarup Nanda of Leadstart Publications. The Leadstart team then took forward the work. My sincere thanks to each of them.

Mental health is as much a concern for all of us as physical health, and mental illness can often be treated and managed. The lack of understanding about mental health results in a social stigma around mental illness. Too often, those with mental illnesses feel isolated. But this need not be so. My hope is that this book will cast a ray of light on those who need help, whether for themselves or for their loved ones.

No voice divine the storm allay'd,
No light propitious shone;
When, snatch'd from all effectual aid,
We perish'd, each alone:
But I beneath a rougher sea,
And whelm'd in deeper gulfs than he.

~ William Cowper
"The Castaway"

1

Aditya's intercom buzzed. It was Aruna, his receptionist.

'Sir, your next patient is here.'

Puzzled, Aditya glanced at the clock. It was 1 pm – time for lunch; there were usually no appointments at this hour.

'Who is it?' he asked.

'Her name is Tanushree Mallick, Sir.'

Tanushree! Yes, of course, she was Dr Rao's referral. When he had been negotiating the crazy Bangalore traffic to get to his Jayanagar clinic that morning, Dr Rao, once his favourite college professor, had called to request him to see a patient immediately. Aditya knew he had a busy day ahead of him but he could not turn down Dr Rao's request. He agreed to see the patient on his own time that afternoon. Usually this was when he spent time reading, documenting reports and putting his thoughts together on different cases. The time was sacred to him and he did not like to give up any part of it, except on rare occasions. Like today.

'But isn't the appointment for 2 pm, Aruna?' he asked now.

'Yes, Sir. But the patient has already turned up and wants to know if you can see her now. I told her you were busy but she is most insistent,' Aruna replied in a hushed tone.

Aditya stopped eating his sandwich, put aside the scattered papers he was working on and quickly scanned his inbox. Dr Rao had said he would send the patient's case history right away. He probably had, but the email was buried somewhere under a pile of junk medical mails. He'd have to search for it later.

'Send her in, Aruna.'

The door opened and a strikingly beautiful young woman walked into the room and smiled at him.

'Good afternoon, Doctor. I'm Tanushree. Thank you for accommodating me at such short notice. Dr Rao told me to be here at 2, but I have a very important meeting at 2:30, which I really can't miss. It's at the other end of town, in Whitefield. That's why I took a chance and came early. It's kind of you to see me.'

Though he did not show it, Aditya was rather perplexed by Tanushree's exuberance. Usually, his new patients were wary and apprehensive when they came to see him. He could not remember if he had ever seen anyone talk so much with a psychiatrist at their first meeting.

Tanushree sensed his bafflement and quickly asked, 'Did I catch you at a bad time, Doctor?'

'No, not at all.' Aditya pushed his lunch aside.

This did not escape Tanushree. In an embarrassed voice, she said, 'Oh my God, I interrupted your lunch! I'm so sorry.'

'There's nothing to be sorry about. I just have a sandwich for lunch anyway. It can wait,' Aditya replied dismissively.

'But...' Suddenly Tanushree's face brightened. She pulled out a plastic box from the big brown bag she was carrying. Opening the lid she offered the contents to him. 'Here, Doctor, please have a piece of my walnut cake.'

Aditya was taken aback. He was a reserved man even in his interactions with familiar people in social settings, and here was a perfect stranger –possibly a patient – offering him food. Aditya did not know how to react.

'Thanks, but I really don't eat cakes or desserts,' he finally mumbled.

But Tanushree was insistent. 'Please Doctor, have a small piece. It's homemade. My mother-in-law herself baked it this morning.'

Aditya curbed his irritation. To discourage further conversation on the subject he broke off a small piece of cake and put it in his mouth. Hmm, it wasn't bad at all.

Somewhat abruptly, Tanushree too, picked up a piece of cake and started eating. 'Isn't it delicious? My mother-in-law makes the most amazing cakes. When Rajeev and I got married four years ago, I had fleetingly mentioned that I was fond of cakes. And ever since, she bakes something for me almost every week.'

'That's really nice,' Aditya said, observing her.

'Doctor, how can you say it's nice?' Tanushree was indignant. 'My mother-in-law looks after the house and our young daughter. Should she really be putting so much effort into baking cakes? Isn't it too much for an elderly lady?'

'You're right,' Aditya agreed easily, wondering why she had come to see him. Was she suffering from some mental ailment? What had bothered Dr Rao so much that he had insisted Aditya see her right away?

Tanushree's eyes softened as she spoke. 'Our daughter, Rini, is three years old. I have not seen a more active child! Forget me, even my husband Rajeev finds it difficult to handle her. Of course, he's busy with his work; he's a software engineer and spends 15 to 20 days a month travelling abroad. And my life is spent shuttling between Bangalore and Chennai on work. So it is my mother-in-law who shoulders the responsibility of managing things at home.'

Aditya waited patiently.

Tanushree took a deep breath and then said, 'Let me tell you why I'm here. I've come to discuss my mother-in-law's health. Rajeev and I tell her to take it easy, but she doesn't listen to anyone. Now she's not in the best of health and has many medical issues. Still, she doesn't seem to care. That's why I go to Dr Rao occasionally to discuss her problems. But this time he insisted I meet you. He said you would definitely be able to help me.'

Aditya was surprised. Why had Dr Rao, an experienced specialist, directed her to him? Why had he sent her to a psychiatrist for what seemed like ancillary geriatric issues? Or did the mother-in-law show symptoms of a psychiatric disorder? Now that was a possibility.

Tanushree noticed that Aditya was distracted. 'I hope I haven't inconvenienced you, Doctor,' she said gently.

'No, not at all. But you'll have to start from the beginning and tell me everything in detail.'

'Sure,' Tanushree responded swiftly. 'Before we begin, could I wash my hands, please?'

'Yes, of course. There is a restroom near the reception. You can ask Aruna, she will show you.'

The moment Tanushree stepped out of the room Aditya searched his inbox for Dr Rao's email. When he located it, he immediately clicked it open. It was important to know what Dr Rao's concerns were before discussing her mother-in-law's health with Tanushree.

The introductory mail from Dr Rao was brief. It said there was no problem with Tanushree's mother-in-law. In fact, there was no mother-in-law, no Rajeev, and no Rini.

Tanushree was not married.

2

After weeks of investigative and emotionally draining sessions, Aditya found that Tanushree's psychiatric disorder had its shards of flawed genes, but they were magnified by childhood trauma. Parental separation had indirectly put her in harm's way of being mentally, physically and sexually abused by her stepfather for years.

Aditya confirmed his suspicion about Tanushree's diagnosis through the slow process of exclusion. Hers was not a simple case of psychosis. Though it was neither his most complex case nor a completely untreatable one, Aditya knew that medicines would not be enough to help Tanushree. It was going to take time and hard work. He was ready for the battle, but the challenge was in also keeping her engaged in the battlefield. Sometimes, he found *that* to be a bigger concern than the ailment itself. So he was happy when Tanushree agreed to come in for consultation once every three weeks.

As Aditya sat at his mahogany desk after his last appointment of the day, his mind wandered back to Tanushree. Absent-mindedly, he pulled a few patient files towards him that Aruna had neatly kept on one corner of his table. The files were his cases for the next day. Soon, he was engrossed in them. He didn't realise how long it was until the phone rang.

'Hello.'

'I don't believe this. You are still in the clinic.' It was his wife Prachi; she did not sound happy.

'Well, someone should always be in attendance for my lady's call,' he quipped.

Aditya's flippant answer annoyed her.

'Stop it. Rekha Aunty has asked us to reach her house by 7:30 this evening. Look at the time. It is seven already. I've been waiting for you at home and you're still there. How will we reach on time?'

Good question. But was it important to reach on time? Was it even necessary to drive to Malleswaram through the traffic and attend the phony party? Aditya would so love to get back home to Koramangala and relax with a glass of red wine.

'You can't get out of this one,' Prachi said firmly, reading his thoughts.

Aditya groaned, knowing that there was no escape.

'Okay, can you get to her house on your own, Prachi? I'll leave right away and come there directly. I may be a little late, but I'll get there.'

'Oh, you're impossible. Hmm, let me see if I can catch a ride with someone. I don't want to drive now, especially not in these clothes. But wait, how can you attend the party in your work clothes?'

'It doesn't matter. No one looks at a man's clothes. Since you are dressed to impress, it will be enough. Tell me, what are you wearing? A sari?'

Prachi was irritated with him.

'Do you really care?' she snapped. 'I'm wearing a swimsuit.'

Aditya couldn't resist.

'Is it one-piece or a bikini?'

'Shut up! You're terrible,' she laughed. 'Don't be too late, alright?'

'I won't.'

'See you soon.' She disconnected the call.

Aditya put the files inside a drawer, locked it, and pushed back his swivel chair. He would have to come in a little early next morning to go through the files, but that was fine. If there was one place that he loved being as much as his study at home, it was his chamber.

His clinic was not a ritzy place in an upscale neighbourhood of Bangalore, but it was spacious and well laid out. The reception area was inviting and there was adequate space for the patients to wait. The door to the left led to his chamber. Just the right size – a cheerful, reassuring space. There was his big desk, lovingly chosen by Prachi, a large bookshelf picked out from a second-hand antique dealer and a lovely wooden Ganesha on a pedestal – a gift from his mother, when he started his private practice. Two paintings bought from a students' exhibition at Karnataka Chitrakala Parishad adorned the wall and that completed the picture.

Aditya straightened one of the paintings, which had become a little lopsided and stepped into the reception area. It was always neat – magazines in the right place, cushions arranged aesthetically, a clean receptionist's desk. Aruna is very organised, Aditya thought appreciatively as he stepped out of his clinic and locked the main door.

Now to Malleswaram. To Rekha Aunty's house. Aditya hated the idea of going to a party, any party, where he would have to deal with fake smiles and catered food. And this time there was the additional burden of dealing with an absurd occasion. He had tried to wriggle out of it as he had done many times earlier, but this once Rekha Aunty was insistent and made an emotional pitch. Finally, Aditya had to give in to the lady, his sole relative in Bangalore and the only person in the entire family who really embarrassed him.

As he walked to his car he remembered Rekha Aunty's maiden trip to Nevada, USA, a few years ago to visit her daughter and son-in-law. When she returned six months later, she had an American twang and her Odia – the only language she spoke except for a smattering of words in Hindi and Kannada – was jarringly interspersed with typical American expressions. Since then, her dinner parties were celebrations of Halloween, Thanksgiving and Christmas. But today's reason was the limit: it was a graduation party for her six-year-old granddaughter Debjani, who had just finished playschool! Aditya hated such frivolous demands on his time.

He got into his car, started the engine and rolled down his window. Just as he was about to drive away a scooter stopped in front of his car. The stocky rider removed his helmet, ran his fingers through his thin hair and looked intently at the signboard on the clinic door.

'Hi, can I help you?'

The man turned, stared at Aditya for a moment and then a big smile lit up his face.

'Aditya? Hi.'

'Hi.' Aditya hesitated. The face was somewhat familiar, but he couldn't put a name to the face in the flickering street light.

'Don't you recognise me?' the man said, as he got down from the scooter and walked closer.

'I'm really sorry, but …'

'I know I've gained weight and lost most of my hair, but I can't believe you've forgotten me. Come on, you Loony Doctor.'

It was a bolt from the blue! Only one person in the world had ever called him 'Loony Doctor' in that playful voice, with a twinkle in his eye.

But it couldn't be him, could it? Aditya stared at him. of course *it* was he! There was no doubt about it. The transformation was dramatic, but it was he alright.

Aditya jumped out of the car and hugged him.

'Prakash! Where have you been all these years? It's so good to see you.'

'It's good to see you too.' There was a slight catch in his voice.

'I thought I would meet you at the last college reunion – after all it was the seventy-fifth year of the college, but I did not see you there. I did meet many of our old friends. Someone told me that you have moved back to Chennai after being in a cardiac hospital in Kuwait for a number of years,' Aditya said animatedly.

'True. These days I work for the government hospital there.'

'That's nice… Prakash, I am extremely sorry for not recognising you right away. The light is so low here.'

'Can't really blame the light. Age hasn't been my friend.'

'Come on, nineteen years is a long time. One's appearance changes. I've changed too.'

'Hardly. The years have been very kind to you. You've still got your good looks and a full head of hair. Apart from a few strands of grey, you look almost the same. Not a wrinkle. Not an extra pound of flesh,' Prakash said seriously.

Aditya was embarrassed.

'Enough… Let's go inside and chat. There is a hell of a lot to catch up.'

'No, not now.' Prakash hesitated. 'You must have had a long day. Why don't I come in tomorrow morning? I just wanted to check out your clinic's location today, and was planning to drop by tomorrow. I never thought that we'd run into each other like this.'

'Well, I'm really glad that we did. Why don't you come in for a few minutes?' Aditya insisted.

Prakash looked away. 'No, I don't have the time now. I have borrowed this scooter from someone and must return it soon. In any case, a few minutes won't do. The truth is… I really need to talk to you as a psychiatrist.'

It was Aditya's turn to be hesitant. He wasn't sure he should be treating a friend. But 19 years had passed after all, and things were so different now.

'Could we meet tomorrow morning and talk?' Prakash asked.

Aditya quickly made up his mind. 'Sure. Come in at 9 am. My first appointment is at 10.'

'I will. Thanks.'

'Bye, Prakash.'

This time they just shook hands. There were no hugs.

3

'Y ou are late, Aditya,' Rekha complained.

'I'm sorry, Aunty. I ran into someone and got delayed.'

'Was it a patient?' she asked curiously. Like many, she was very curious about the world of mental disorders. It was somewhat voyeuristic – Aditya didn't like that.

'No, it was an old friend.' Aditya swiftly ended the interrogation.

'You are always late for parties. You aren't the only doctor in the city, you know. Look at Nikki's husband. He's a doctor too, but he's punctual and manages his time really well…'

Here we go again, Aditya thought. He dreaded Rekha Aunty's repetitive stories of her perfect son-in-law.

'Aunty, where is Debjani?' he interjected. 'I must congratulate her first.'

Rekha beamed.

'Oh yes, of course! After all, the party is for Jenny.' She looked around and pointed out the six year old.

'There she is – standing next to the cake. Doesn't she look so-o-o pretty today?'

Aditya nodded dutifully and walked away. After congratulating a somewhat distracted Debjani, he glanced around the room, desperately searching for his wife. He spotted her having an animated conversation with a flamboyantly dressed lady.

As soon as Prachi saw him, she came over.

'You are really late. Everyone is here and Debjani is about to cut the cake.'

'Good, then we can go back home quickly.'

'You are incorrigible,' Prachi whispered, hoping that nobody had heard Aditya's comment. 'Well? What happened? Why are you late?'

'I met someone on my way here.'

'Who?'

'Prakash.'

'Prakash! After all these years!' Prachi touched her husband's hand involuntarily. She was concerned.

'Why did he meet you?' she asked.

'I don't think he had planned to. We just ran into each other as I was leaving the clinic. Maybe he was thinking through whether to actually go ahead and meet me or not.'

'But why? What did he say?'

Aditya shrugged.

'Nothing much. He said that he needed to talk to me as a psychiatrist. He'll meet me in my office tomorrow morning…'

Their conversation was drowned by a high-pitched announcement; it was Rekha. For the next few minutes, she delivered a glorious description of Debjani's achievements in playschool and her future prospects at a prestigious and, of course, expensive international school. Aditya saw Debjani getting fidgety; it was torturous for her to keep watching the cake and not bite into it. Thankfully, the speech ended and the cake was cut amidst applause and another round of congratulatory words.

Aditya sighed with relief. Now at least they could grab some dinner and leave.

On the way home in the car, Prachi tried to draw Aditya into a conversation about the guests at the party.

'Do you know that Shankar and Rina are planning to buy their daughter an apartment in Pune?'

Aditya shook his head.

'Oh, I almost forgot. Deben's mother has developed a heart condition. Can you talk to Dr Nair and set up an appointment for her? She's only sixty-five…' Her voice trailed off when she realised that her husband probably wasn't listening.

That was true. Aditya was lost in his thoughts. Why did Prakash seek him out after all these years, when they had practically no communication at all? If he needed to see a psychiatrist, he could have found one in Chennai, where he was now a cardiologist. Why come to Bangalore looking for one? Was stigma a factor here? Unlikely, though. Prakash had always been pragmatic and rational; he could not have changed so drastically. There had to be some other reason. He would have to wait till morning to find that out.

***

Next morning, Prakash reached the clinic on time. He sat down on a chair opposite Aditya and somewhat awkwardly said:

'Deepa is in Bangalore now.'

Aditya's heart missed a beat. Deepa? Why was

Prakash bringing up her name? Why talk about something that had shattered trust, friendship and his heart a long time ago?

It had all happened during his medical college days. The memory was now faded, the pain dulled, the scar receded. But in a flash, everything came back.

When he had first arrived in the college town, hundreds of miles away from a metro, Aditya felt like he had walked into the dilapidated sets of a black-and-white movie. The arid landscape, monotonous buildings and dreary surroundings dampened his spirits. His disappointment with the town intensified when he stepped into his assigned room in the boys' hostel and saw the personal belongings of his new roommate kept in a corner. There was an old-fashioned trunk, a tattered hold-all and, resting against that, was a stainless-steel tiffin-carrier. All these portrayed a picture of an uncool, straitlaced person and Aditya dreaded the prospect of sharing a room for an entire year with someone like that.

Just then, that someone walked in. One look at his nondescript clothes, well-worn brown sandals and oily hair filled Aditya's mind with disdain and he was convinced that behind the small town get-up lay a mediocre personality.

'Are you Aditya?' his roommate asked with a smile.

Aditya nodded, gingerly taking out his guitar. He wanted to avoid any conversation.

'I'm Prakash. When did you arrive?'

'Maybe an hour ago,' Aditya said briefly, strumming his guitar.

'But no bus reaches at that time,' Prakash continued.

Aditya was irritated. Anybody else in Prakash's shoes would have taken the hint by now – that he wanted to be left alone.

'I came by taxi from Chennai.'

'Oh, that must have been expensive.'

Aditya was tempted to snap at him – Shut up, you blabbermouth. Instead he just strummed louder.

Thankfully, there were no more curious questions from his roommate, who quietly sat down on his bed and concentrated on a crossword puzzle.

When Aditya finally put the guitar down, Prakash looked up, smiled as before and said:

'You play the guitar really well.'

'Thanks,' Aditya mumbled. Maybe he should not have been so curt. But the next question from his roommate evoked his earlier irritation.

'Have you had lunch yet?' Prakash asked.

What a stupid question! How did it matter to him whether he'd had lunch or not?

'Yes, I ate with my Dad,' Aditya said, as he pretended to unpack his suitcase.

'Your father is here?' Prakash was very excited. 'You know, my father also wanted to come, but something came up at the last minute. You are lucky… Aditya, may I meet your father? I would love to take his blessings.'

Aditya could not imagine any of his friends from the city ever wanting to meet his father for his blessings. Who does that these days?

'Sure, you can meet him when he comes.' His voice was brusque.

Aditya's father had gone to meet one of his friends, who was a professor in that medical college and soon returned to his son's room. To Aditya's surprise, he started a conversation with Prakash right away. Maybe he was just making sure that his son wasn't in bad company, Aditya thought with a smirk. His smirk, however, soon gave way to amazement, when he saw his rather reserved father carry on a long and warm conversation with his roommate. He wondered what he saw in

Prakash that made him discuss his family, school and future aspirations.

'I'm glad that you have a nice roommate. He's really pleasant, genuine and smart,' his father said, when he finally walked out from the room.

Before long, Aditya realised that Prakash was everything that his father had said he was. That small-town boy from a lower-middle-class family was sincere and unaffected. What really endeared him to Aditya was the fact that although he had very high moral standards for himself, Prakash wasn't judgemental about others. Soon, both of them became very close – almost inseparable.

***

Classes started. Aditya had assumed that with his intellect and background, medical academia would be a breeze. After all, his grandfather had a successful hospital in Cuttack and he literally grew up in its backyard, listening in to regular discussions of myriad health issues. It didn't quite turn out that way. The professors, with nothing else to do in that godforsaken college town, made the students slog to prepare them for the tough years ahead. Aditya found it difficult to keep up to speed. He even toyed with the idea of an alternative career in music, despite limited talent.

Unlike him, Prakash seemed much more at ease. His constant encouragement and endless cups of coffee brewed on a rickety stove in one corner of the room slowly helped Aditya to cope. He was grateful that finally he had managed to find a true friend, who unlike him was always steady; nothing ruffled him.

That was why Aditya was taken aback, when a flustered and distraught Prakash barged into the room on a particular Saturday and blurted out:

'My uncle has come to this town on a transfer along with his family.'

'So?'

'I have to go and meet them.'

'So meet them.'

Prakash plopped himself on the bed.

'It is not that simple, Aditya. You have no idea about our relatives and the ugly family politics…'

The sordid family tale came out.

'You know, my father had a flourishing business; he managed three grocery stores. One day, my mother's eldest brother arrived. He had lost his job. His family was starving. Without a second thought, my father asked my uncle to manage one of his stores. After a few days, my mother's youngest brother landed up with a similar sob story. Again, my father gave him the charge of another store. These two uncles turned out to be swindlers; they took advantage of my father's simplicity and completely duped him.'

'Your father did not go to the police?'

'He could have, if he had wanted. But then, he thought that my mother's family would be disgraced and that might hurt my mother. He just asked both my uncles to leave. He did not create a furore. The family should have been grateful, but on the contrary, they took offence. Nobody ever sympathised with the fact that my father's business was ruined; he could never build it back… After that, there has been no love lost between the two sides.'

'This uncle who has shifted here is your mother's brother?'

'No, his wife is my mother's older sister.'

'Were they involved in the swindling?'

'No, no – not at all. In fact they always kept away from family politics, as this uncle was posted in some remote place.'

'Then why are you so upset that they are here?'

'I don't like anybody from my mother's side any more… How on earth did they know that I am here? And even if they do, why write to me and invite me home? The only time they saw me was probably when I was a baby.'

'Maybe they always knew what your father went through and have felt bad. And in their own way, they are trying to reach out.'

'Maybe…' Prakash continued, 'I wrote to my father about it. I thought he would tell me to ignore my uncle's invitation. But both my parents feel that I should visit them.'

'So do it. Tomorrow is a Sunday. Go and meet them in the morning.'

'Will you come with me?'

Aditya felt awkward with the strange request, but then he could not refuse Prakash.

***

Come Sunday morning, the two friends went to Prakash's uncle's house with some trepidation. Prakash walked up to the main door of the small house and knocked gingerly. A young woman draped in an ordinary, pale-pink, cotton sari opened the door. She was tall, dusky and delicate. Her long hair was tied in a bun with a few escaped strands at the nape. She wore a simple chain and a pair of old-fashioned ruby studs adorned her ears. There was no makeup on her face – just a small black *bindi* on the forehead. Her oval face was pretty, but it was really the blue-green eyes that were mesmerising.

Aditya found it difficult to tear his eyes away; he had no idea that a woman could be so attractive.

Prakash introduced himself. She gasped and then ran inside, leaving the two young men, confused, at the doorstep. In a moment, an older couple came out. Prakash walked up to them and touched their feet. The awkwardness and anxiety just melted away.

Originally, Aditya and Prakash had planned to just say hello, probably have a cup of tea, make some polite conversation and get back to the hostel before lunch. But things did not quite happen that way.

'Deepa, get them something to eat first.'

'We had a late breakfast. Just a cup of tea would be fine.' Prakash tried to be polite.

Just as the four of them settled down to chat about the new place, parents, life at the college and the hostel, Deepa returned with a tray loaded with snacks.

Aditya's eyes took in the mouth-watering fare, but he also tried to be polite like his friend.

'There is no way we can eat so much,' he said.

'Of course you can,' Deepa said with a twinkle. 'I know perfectly well the kind of breakfast you get in a hostel. I am sure you are starving.'

Aditya loved the way she dismissed their protest: she had genuine warmth. Frankly, they were famished. The morning breakfast of *idlis* and insipid chutney had been digested a long time back. The two demolished everything that was served on the plate. Then came coffee. The boys were happy and ready to get back to their hostel.

'How can I let you go without lunch?' Prakash's aunt said in a horrified voice.

'Aunty, we have a test tomorrow. Lots of studying to do. We will come again.'

'You can do the studying in the evening. I am making a special mutton curry today. You have to have lunch here.' This was Deepa. It had been months since Aditya and Prakash had home-style mutton curry; the once-a-week, spicy, oily, over-cooked mutton curry served in the hostel was a far cry from what they had left behind to study medicine.

After an elaborate lunch later that afternoon, even as Prakash's uncle and aunt excused themselves for an afternoon nap, Aditya and Prakash, instead of heading back to the hostel, just lingered on. The three of them talked about many things: the university, the Durga Puja, this town's terrible heat and, of course, the place Deepa's family had just relocated from, after living there for many years.

'It must have been terribly boring to spend so many years in a village. How did you manage?' This was Aditya.

'No, it wasn't. Have you ever been to that part of India? To Madhugiri?'

'No… Is that the name of the village? What a strange name! Madhugiri – honey hill. Wow!'

'It is a very beautiful place. If you had ever been there, you wouldn't make fun of it.'

Aditya was not prepared to lose the argument.

'I might not have heard the name of the village, but I have read enough about the district. It is the back of beyond: roads are bad, there is hardly any good place to stay, and there is no communication. And what do you do there? Just look at the greenery and get bitten by mosquitoes?'

'I agree,' Prakash concurred.

'This is what happens to people like you who live in cities. Have you ever seen fireflies at night?

Have you ever walked barefoot on the green grass wet with morning dew? Have you ever bathed under a waterfall?'

'I thought the last one was the prerogative of Bollywood heroines,' Prakash said with a straight face and was promptly whacked on the head by Deepa.

Family ties are strange, Aditya thought. It bonds people so quickly. Come to think of it, just a few hours back Prakash had hardly known Deepa's family.

'You have no idea how calming nature can be. I was so upset when my father got transferred.'

'But didn't you spend your entire school life in hostels in some other town?'

'Yes, I did. But Madhugiri was home. That kept me going… And now this dreary town.' She sighed.

Aditya was touched. On an impulse, he said, 'I will go to Madhugiri one day; I have to check out the place. It actually sounds quite nice.'

'I will come along,' Prakash added.

Deepa beamed.

'Are you serious? You must let me know when you go. I will come and show you around.'

Their animated discussion had to end soon. Prakash's uncle was up from his afternoon siesta and demanded some tea.

'Sure, *Acha.*' Deepa rushed to the kitchen to make tea for everybody.

The tea was repeated at six. This time with a big spread of snacks. Prakash and Aditya's dinner was literally taken care of.

***

The two were invited again the next Sunday. Soon, spending Sundays at Prakash's aunt's house was routine. The pressure at the medical college and the unpalatable hostel food became manageable because they knew the weekend would be coming soon.

Prakash's uncle went to the market early every Sunday to get all the good stuff the boys liked, his aunt cooked the most delectable dishes and Deepa served all this with a lot of warmth. After the lunch they always had interesting conversation; everyone got more and more comfortable as time went by.

'You know, Aditya,' Prakash exclaimed one day as they were returning to their hostel after a day at his aunt's, 'I had no idea I would get so attached to them in three months. Being with Aunty is like being with my mother; Uncle is even more peace-loving and modest than my father; and Deepa... I sometimes feel she is not my cousin but my sister.'

Aditya said nothing. After three months, he was sure about one thing. Though he loved Prakash's uncle and aunty like his own, he had no brotherly feelings for Deepa; he was totally enamoured by her. She was beautiful, and more importantly, had an amazingly sharp mind. In fact, when he first discovered that she was a student of English literature, he was quite surprised. Somehow, he could not connect English literature with someone from a village like Madhugiri.

An entire year went by and Aditya's crush on Deepa soon transformed into a deep attraction.

Aditya clearly remembered the day; everything was closed because of a local festival. The weather, though cloudy, had an expectant note about it. There was something magical in the air. Prakash and Aditya landed up at Deepa's house.

It turned out to be very much a repeat of the Sundays – the great food, the predictable siesta of the parents, and their leisurely conversation. The three sat in a quiet corner of the cool veranda with trees on three sides. After some time, Prakash started yawning and soon had difficulty keeping his eyes open. The great lunch had taken effect.

'I need to nap for a while.'

'Go to my room,' Deepa said.

There was a lull in the conversation after Prakash left; an awkwardness between two people that neither knew how to handle.

'Let me make some ginger tea.' She stood up.

'No, you don't have to go.' On an impulse, Aditya leaned across and pulled Deepa's hand. She lost her balance and fell clumsily on the mat right next to him. He did not know what happened, but the next moment, he quickly took her in his arms and kissed her. Deepa kissed him back; the longing and the passion shook both of them to the core.

It felt like an eternity. But instinctively, she pulled back, a look of alarm on her face.

'Please, please, don't discuss this with Prakash.'

'Why, Deepa? I love you.'

'I know. I love you too, Aditya. But... you will not understand.'

'What will I not understand?' Aditya was baffled.

'Please don't insist.' Her lips quivered. The lovely eyes threatened to brim over.

'Okay. I will keep it a secret, our secret, till you become comfortable,' Aditya said as she slid out of his arms.

***

Time flew by. Soon, it was time for their third-year exams. One day, while they were studying together, Prakash said:

'Oh, by the way, there is some good news. Deepa's wedding date has been finalised. I met Uncle today when I had gone to town for a haircut and he told me.'

Aditya looked at him in disbelief.

'She's so lucky,' Prakash added. 'She's moving to London immediately after the wedding.'

Aditya continued to stare at him; the shock and pain was all over his face. The truth dawned on Prakash all of a sudden; he realised that his best friend had been in love with his cousin.

'God, Aditya, you should have told me.'

Prakash held his head between his hands.

'I had no idea you felt this way. Aunty once told me that Deepa got engaged soon after she completed high school. You know how conservative our families are. Her parents wanted to get her married within a few months after the engagement, but the groom went to London for further studies and they had to wait. He's started working recently and his family has requested the wedding date to be set. Now I understand why Deepa was so distraught and upset with this development.'

'Can't you do something?' Aditya pleaded.

Prakash looked away. How could he argue with Deepa's parents? Besides, it wasn't going to be easy to break off a wedding that was promised years ago. It would lead to social boycott in his community and ruin the family reputation. Aditya was a big-city boy and from a different cultural upbringing; he wouldn't understand these things.

And Aditya didn't. He resented Prakash for not helping him.

The next day, Aditya received a letter from Deepa – a letter with just two lines. There was no explanation and no apology. Deepa simply broke up with him.

Days went by with only one change in his routine. Aditya joined a yoga class on Sundays and with that excuse, he stopped going to Deepa's house.

In due course, he received the wedding invitation. Thankfully, the venue was Trivandrum because the groom's family had settled there. Aditya was relieved. A medical student was not expected to take time off to attend an outstation wedding. In fact, as they had their practical only a few days later, even Prakash was unable to travel to Trivandrum.

Soon after Deepa's wedding, Prakash's uncle was transferred back to Madhugiri. Aditya heaved a sigh of relief. He did not have to endure the yoga classes any more.

After that incident, Prakash and Aditya drifted apart. They tried to be cordial, but something wasn't quite right. Nonetheless, they remained roommates until college was over. But they never discussed anything personal.

***

Aditya returned to the present and was puzzled. Why was Prakash bringing up Deepa's name now, after all this time?

Prakash cleared his throat. He was quite uncomfortable talking about the past. But he plodded on.

'After Deepa got married, she hardly called her parents from London. Every few years, she would come to India for a week. And when she was here, she remained aloof and withdrawn. We thought that London had changed her. Time went by and nine years back, when Deepa's mother passed away, her father was heartbroken. Deepa came to India for her mother's last rites, but went back to London just a few days later. Her phone calls to her father continued to be as infrequent as before. In the meantime, Uncle retired and decided to move to Bangalore. He has some close relatives here, but still he was very lonely. I tried to reach out to Deepa to talk about her father but she wouldn't reply to my emails. The truth is that she hasn't really talked to me properly ever since she broke up with you...'

'Why are you telling me all this?' Aditya was getting impatient.

'Three years ago, Deepa's husband died.'

'What!'

'Yes, it was a huge shock for all of us. I immediately booked my ticket for London, but Deepa didn't want anybody to come there. The last rites were done in London by her and later, she just sent her husband's ashes through a close family friend. That's when her father realised that Deepa had stayed aloof for a reason; something had been amiss in her marriage all these years.'

'Why do you say that?'

'It was probably a hunch. Anyway, Uncle did his best to persuade her to come, live here with him. He renovated his Bangalore home to make it suitable for Deepa and her son, but she had no intention of returning. She stayed on in London until her fourteen-year-old son Raj became a problem.'

'Teenage problem?' Aditya asked.

'I don't think so. It seems to be something more than that. Raj was a brilliant student all along. But gradually, his grades slipped and apparently, he was becoming aggressive at home. Then Deepa started getting complaints from school and soon, he became unmanageable. That's when Deepa decided to return to Bangalore with the hope that a change of place would do the boy some good.' Prakash paused. 'But according to Deepa, there is no improvement. Somewhat reluctantly, she let me spend some time with Raj and my intuition says that he needs help.'

'What kind of help?'

Prakash said rather slowly, 'Deepa hasn't told me anything, but I think Raj has a psychological problem.'

'Hmmm.' Aditya thought for a while. 'But I rarely see children. You should talk to Dr Nandi. He's one of the best child psychiatrists in the city and has a clinic in Indiranagar.'

'Yes, I remember Nandi. He was a year senior to us in medical college. But…'

'I'll be happy to call and talk to him about Raj before you take him there,' Aditya offered.

'No, Aditya, that's not needed at all. I can't take Raj to Dr Nandi.'

Aditya looked at Prakash quizzically.

'Why not?'

'Deepa has to be persuaded first.'

'What do you mean?'

'She refuses to accept that Raj may have a psychological problem. That's why I want you to see him and then talk to Deepa. Hopefully, she'll listen to you.'

'But Prakash, you aren't just a doctor; you are also her cousin. You should be able to explain it to her. After all, I am an outsider.' Aditya emphasised the last word.

Prakash persisted. 'If anyone can convince her, it's you. She's always respected you.'

Aditya felt uncomfortable. 'Come on, Prakash. That was 22 years ago.'

'Does that mean that you won't see Raj?'

'Sure I will, if you think it will help. When do you want to bring him here?' Aditya replied, trying to sound professional.

Prakash hesitated, not sure how to say it.

'Do you think that you can come with me to Deepa's house?'

Aditya wasn't ready for this – it was stretching things too far.

Before he could reply, Prakash pleaded with him:

'Please, Aditya. I have tried to convince Deepa many times, but she's in denial. I'm hoping that she will assume that your visit is purely social, which will lower her guard and hopefully, you can influence her to get professional help for her son before it is too late.'

'She's not a fool,' Aditya wanted to say. Deepa would instantly know the reason for his visit, though there was a chance that she would cooperate. After all, it was for her son's well-being. He said, 'Okay, I'll come with you.'

'What about today?' Prakash asked. 'Maybe in the evening, after your clinic hours? I'm going back tomorrow.'

'That's fine. We can leave from here at 6 p.m.'

***

Hours later, Aditya was ready when Prakash came to the clinic in an auto-rickshaw and peeped into his room.

'Shall we go?'

'Yes.' Aditya left a few housekeeping instructions with Aruna and stepped out with Prakash.

The two men walked silently to the car and soon, they were on their way to Deepa's father's house. The roads were congested with cars, two-wheelers, cyclists, pedestrians, cows and dogs. Everybody seemed to be in a hurry. Aditya made his way carefully through the traffic.

As the car stopped at a signal, Prakash asked:

'Do you want to ask me anything else about Deepa or Raj?'

Aditya didn't want to talk about Raj or Deepa.

'You think anyone can have a conversation while driving through this terrible traffic? Driving in Bangalore has become a nightmare. I'm seriously thinking of hiring a driver.'

Prakash ignored Aditya's response.

'I want you to know something. We think that Deepa's husband Naren committed suicide.'

Aditya glanced at Prakash. This one had taken him quite by surprise.

'Of course, there is no proof. And Deepa told us a different story.'

'What story?'

'She said that Naren was waiting for a train when it happened. That particular day, he was running late for work. While waiting at the station, he became giddy and fell onto the tracks... Now I am not sure whether he fell down accidentally or he intentionally jumped in front of the train. Whatever it might have been, my suspicion is that Naren's violent death had a disturbing effect on his son. Raj is fourteen years old now, but at times, he behaves like a small child and babbles.'

'What does Deepa think about that? Hasn't she noticed that something's wrong?'

'I'm sure that she has and must be very concerned, but she refuses to see the truth. She is clearly in denial.'

'Most people do that. The problem has to be explained to her in a proper way. Only a family member can...'

'Ah, here we are!' Prakash interrupted. 'This is the house. You can park anywhere.'

Aditya carefully parked his car under a young banyan tree. While locking the car, his eyes went over the facade of the house. It was small and unpretentious. At one time, the house had probably been beige with dark-brown accents and matching windows, but years of neglect had turned it into muddied yellow with lines of black fungus reaching down from the top to meet splotches of green algae near the bottom. The brown windows were worn and the warped wood just about managed to hold.

The tiny garden in the front was a contrast. Even in the low light of the evening, Aditya could see that it was blooming and seemed well cared for. It had Deepa's signature all over it.

His eyes glanced over the house again and strayed to the unfinished terrace. That was when Aditya saw an unfamiliar figure standing in one corner. It was dusk, the streetlights were not switched on and yet, he instantly knew it was her.

When Prakash rang the doorbell, she came down to open the door.

'Come in.' Deepa held the door open. She hadn't noticed Aditya yet. The streaks of white in the once gloriously dark brown hair were startling.

'Deepa, look who's here.'

She looked at the man walking in behind Prakash. There was a moment of awkward silence as a flicker of recognition crossed her eyes.

'Aditya? Is that really you?'

Aditya tried to smile.

'I can't believe you recognised me after all these years.'

'You haven't changed a bit!'

Aditya wished he could say the same about her – there was absolutely no similarity with the girl whom he had known in the springtime of his life. He wondered what had ravaged her lithe body, damaged that delicate skin and dulled her mesmerising blue-green eyes. The lady in front of him was overweight and appeared much older than him. It couldn't just be age; it had to be something more than that.

'I met Prakash yesterday and he asked me to come,' Aditya explained, though there was no reason for him to do so.

'That's so nice. Come in, please.'

Like the house, the living room had seen better days. There was an old sofa flanked by two cane chairs.

The curtains on the windows were threadbare; the coffee table was basic and except for the morning newspaper and a couple of old magazines, there was nothing else on it. However, on the centre wall, a *kaduthala* – a curved sword – was proudly displayed. Aditya knew that it belonged to an ancestor who was a *kalaripayattu* warrior some two hundred years back. She had once told him the story of the heirloom.

'This *kaduthala* has travelled all the way to Bangalore?' he exclaimed.

'*Achan* wouldn't let go of this,' Deepa said disinterestedly.

'Why should he? It is, after all, a family heirloom.'

'Well, when families disintegrate, what importance does a rusty sword have?' The words were not like those of the Deepa that Aditya knew.

Before he could reply, she changed the subject.

'So tell me about yourself. How long have you been in Bangalore?'

'Years, now. I came to Bangalore to do my MD and just stayed on.'

'Ah yes, now I remember. Prakash told me a few weeks ago that you have your private clinic here and you are doing very well. I was happy to hear that. What's your specialisation?'

'I am a psychiatrist.'

Deepa gave Prakash a sharp, startled look, who pretended to look nonchalant.

'Do you know that Aditya's wife is a leading paediatrician?' he said casually. 'I remember that you had once asked me if I knew a good one in Bangalore. Maybe you can get her to see Raj.'

Deepa visibly tried to calm herself and spoke to Aditya.

'Why did you switch over to psychiatry? I thought you were more interested in cardiology, like Prakash.'

This was not the time to get into the long story. Aditya's reply was brief.

'I became interested in psychiatry in my final year.'

There was an uncomfortable silence.

Prakash cleared his throat and asked: 'Where's Raj?'

'In his room, where else? He must be playing a video game.'

'Okay, I'll say "hello" to him and be right back.'

Aditya watched him go. He knew why Prakash had left him alone with Deepa.

'How have you been, Deepa?'

'Alive, I guess.'

'Do you like Bangalore after living in London for such a long time?'

'Do I really have an option? It's my fate.'

'I'm surprised. You were never a believer of fate. Remember how you used to disagree with us? Once your mother told you that nobody could win against providence. You were so annoyed that you argued with her the entire afternoon.'

'I did?' Deepa sounded tired. 'Maybe I did. I was young and foolish then.'

Aditya didn't quite know what to say. Deepa abruptly asked:

'Is it true that your wife is a paediatrician?'

Aditya nodded.

'Where does she work? Does she have her own clinic?'

'No, she doesn't. She is at a private hospital.'

'Can she see my son sometime?'

'I'll tell her. When do you want to see her?'

'Whenever she can fit us in. Any day, any time is fine by me.'

'It's the flu season and a lot of children are falling sick.' Aditya was circumspect.

Deepa looked troubled for a moment and said awkwardly:

'No, it's not the flu. Raj lost his father in an accident and I think that has traumatised him. I can see that he's changing – he was a brilliant student before, but he isn't interested in his studies any more. Will your wife really see Raj? He's almost fifteen now. Maybe he's too old?'

'No, not at all, Deepa. Take him to Prachi; I'll fill her in before you meet her. But if you think that Raj's lack of interest in studies and his unwillingness to go to school is because of trauma, then it may be better to consult a psychiatrist. Or at least a counsellor.'

Deepa crossed her arms tightly and her eyes flashed.

'Raj is not mad,' she snapped.

Aditya was relieved – *that was the exact reaction he was waiting for.* It was so much easier to deal with confrontation than passive replies.

'Come on, Deepa. You've stayed in a place like London for so long. You've got to know this: does someone need to be mad in order to see a counsellor? Many perfectly normal people go to them for advice. It's only when a counsellor recommends that one should see a psychiatrist, you go to one. Even then, it doesn't mean you are mad or crazy. Most people are not.'

'I'm not naïve, Aditya. I know when one needs to seek help. I've had enough experience with these things; I've been to hell and back,' she retorted. Sparks of anger remained though she did not explain further.

'I'm sure you have.' Aditya wished that he had asked Prakash more questions on their way in. 'But please know that sometimes there is a minor problem caused by a chemical imbalance and it needs attention. If you ignore it, it's not going to go away like a common cold. It can get aggravated and develop into something chronic that will be more difficult to treat later.'

'There's no such problem with Raj.' Her tone was curt.

'I hope so, but sometimes we tend to overlook subtle symptoms. It's difficult to be pragmatic when it concerns a loved one. If you want, I can…'

'I told you earlier. Raj does not have any such problem.' Deepa's mouth was set in a hard line. She continued to be furious as before. Seconds later, her face twitched and the confrontational air gave way to unshed tears. Deepa collected herself and mumbled, 'Can you please help me, Aditya? Raj is all that I have in this world. He's the only reason for me to live. I don't know what's happened to him… what's happening…If something dreadful occurs…'

Aditya interrupted her. 'Don't think that way, Deepa. Most psychiatric problems can be treated. It needs to be diagnosed correctly, that's all.'

'Will it really help? Naren too…'

'What happened to Naren?'

'It was an accident. He was going to work. As he was waiting at the station, he became unsteady and fell onto the tracks – right in front of an oncoming train…' Deepa said and averted her eyes.

She didn't sound convincing. Aditya immediately knew that the story was fabricated for the world, but he did not react. He knew from experience that the truth would come out sooner or later. The question was how to make it sooner rather than later.

At that moment, Prakash walked into the room.

'Is there something to eat? I'm hungry.'

'Hungry?' Deepa looked blank. Years ago, she would have rushed into the kitchen to come back with a tray full of food. But today, she was hesitant.

'Will biscuits do? I think there is a packet somewhere.'

'I have a better idea. Why don't you make us some tea? I'll run along and bring hot *samosas* and *jalebis* from the new shop down the street. That shop makes delicious stuff.'

'Sure. Do that.' Deepa looked relieved as she went into the kitchen to make tea.

Aditya picked up the morning's newspaper from the coffee table and flipped through it. Life was stranger than fiction. Who could have imagined that he would meet Deepa so many years after, and in such circumstances? And he wasn't even supposed to be a psychiatrist in the first place.

4

Back in the nineteen sixties, Aditya's grandfather had a small hospital in Cuttack. After his death, his three older sons and their wives, all of them doctors, took over the hospital. Subodh, the fourth son, and his wife Minu, were the only exceptions in the family. Subodh was an architect and worked elsewhere, but he helped out the family business whenever the hospital needed expansion or renovation. Minu, a commerce graduate, preferred to be a homemaker. It was a nice arrangement for everyone until the day Subodh went missing just ten months after his marriage.

There was no suspicion of foul play or an accident; it was clear that he had planned his going away from home. Before disappearing, he had added his wife's name to all his bank accounts. The small house in Puri was gifted to her. All his other affairs were carefully sorted out. There was nothing missing except his black briefcase. It was baffling because there was no apparent reason for him to leave. The wedding had his consent. Minu was a nice person and the couple rarely had any disagreements; there was no sign of stress in his professional life nor was another woman in the picture.

The family was in shock. The police was informed, a private detective was employed, and the net was cast far and wide. Days turned into months and months into years. There was no sign of Subodh.

As the family started giving up, Minu began losing interest in everything. She stopped managing the home and stayed in her bedroom all day. Aditya's grandfather wanted her to assist him with administrative tasks at the hospital, but Minu demurred. She was overwhelmed with the idea of interacting with strangers every day. Aditya's grandmother offered to take her to her parents' house in the village, but she refused. The years went by. Though things were never the same, everyone gradually returned to their routine. Minu also recuperated somewhat and resumed her duties. Subodh's nephews and nieces became her responsibility. That was when Aditya grew close to her. It was Minu Aunty who looked after him, disciplined him and pushed him to work hard. Everything was alright.

Until that fateful day. It was the day after the Dussehra festival. All the children had assembled on the terrace in the late evening to watch the fireworks and the procession of Durga idols as they were taken for immersion. Minu was also there, keeping an eye on the children. Even as he was busy watching the Dussehra procession, Aditya noticed Minu standing on the edge and peering down at the ground. She stood there for a long time. But he did not pay much attention to it.

Suddenly there was a loud thud. The children looked around and realised that Minu Aunty had fallen from the terrace. There was a huge commotion and the scared bunch of children rushed down the stairs, screaming. Miraculously, Minu was mostly unhurt. She later said that she had lost her balance while watching the fireworks. Twelve-year-old Aditya was not so sure, even as the other adults accepted her explanation. He, however, decided not to voice his doubts. Soon, the episode was forgotten.

Five years later, there was another incident. Minu was admitted to the hospital when she accidentally swallowed rat poison. Her stomach had to be pumped out. Shocked neighbours had flocked their house. It was a scary time for the family.

'It's my fault. I kept the liquid in a water bottle,' Aditya's teary-eyed grandmother had told everybody. There was no discussion on the subject in front of the children, but they knew that everyone was thinking about one thing – that Minu

Aunty had tried to kill herself. Days later, Minu returned from the hospital, looking quite normal and cheerful. In time, that disturbing incident was also left behind, and while his cousins moved on from the episode, Aditya could not. He couldn't shake off the feeling that something wasn't quite right. He became protective of Minu Aunty and they remained close until the day Aditya left to study medicine.

At the medical college, he got busy with work and Deepa. After Deepa's marriage, he threw himself completely into his studies; there was no time for anything else.

Then one day, he got a call from his father. He was surprised – it wasn't usual for him to call on a weekday.

'Baba, is everything okay?'

'Come home. Minu is not well. Get the first flight you can,' his father replied without any preamble. Aditya sensed that the matter was serious.

He left Prakash a hurried note as he rushed to catch the overnight bus to Chennai from where he would take a flight home. The next evening, when he reached home, he found that Minu Aunty was no longer alive. She had passed away a few hours before his father had called him. Minu Aunty had committed suicide.

Aditya was stunned.

His father spoke to him gently.

'We never told you this, Aditya, but Minu had a psychiatric problem. For years, we had no inkling, thinking that Subodh's disappearance had played havoc with her mind. A few years back, comprehensive tests were done and we discovered that Minu had a serious depressive disorder. Her treatment started and she was under a lot of medication. But obviously, something went wrong somewhere.'

It wasn't entirely a revelation. Aditya had his suspicions when he was younger, though he did not know the facts then. His doubts became stronger when he joined medical college and read up on the subject, but as his own life took precedence over everything else, Minu's affairs were pushed to the back of his mind. Now Aditya was able to connect the dots.

While returning from Cuttack after her last rites, Aditya realised that Minu Aunty's suicide had probably been preventable. Maybe what she had needed was more specialised attention and monitoring. How come a family of doctors did not realise that? Why did it escape their notice? Aditya was deep in thought.

Over the next few days, he gained clarity. There were doctors in his family, but no psychiatrist. That was when he made up his mind. He had to learn more about the human psyche. He would probe, find answers and steer people like Minu Aunty away from tragic outcomes. He had to become a psychiatrist.

After his MBBS, his family tried to discourage him, but Aditya did not change his mind. Aditya's great-grandfather was a 'licensed medical practitioner', an LMP doctor, as they were called back then. His grandfather was a graduate from a medical college, who preferred to be a general practitioner and ran his private hospital. His son, Aditya's father, wanted to be a surgeon, but ended up as a pathologist. Aditya's mother was a dermatologist. When Aditya topped his class, everyone wanted him to specialise in cardiology or orthopaedics. But Aditya stood his ground.

His father tried to reason with him, 'Look, with your grades you have so many other options. Don't you think you should give them serious considerations?'

'No. Baba, I really want to specialise in psychiatry,' Aditya was firm.

'But, why?' Aditya's mother was flummoxed. 'This is going to be your future. Your career. You cannot be impulsive about these things.'

Aditya could not tell her that it was not an impulsive decision – that it was a decision taken months before his graduation and after much mulling over Minu's death.

5

'H_{i.}

Aditya broke out of his reverie as he watched a young boy saunter into the living room with a book in his hands. Deepa's son, no doubt. The boy had his mother's smile, her blue-green eyes and a nice crop of hair.

'Ah, you must be Raj,' Aditya said.

'Yes, I am. And you're Prakash Uncle's friend! He told me that you met each other yesterday after nineteen years,' the boy said in a marked British accent.

'That's true. We were very close friends.'

'Really? Were you best friends?'

'I think so.'

'Then why didn't you see each other more often? I can't stay away from my best friend at all; I have to see him every day.' Raj sat down on a chair and opened his book. But he didn't read it; he was fidgety and appeared distracted. Abruptly, he looked up and smiled at Aditya. It was a friendly smile.

'Tell me, Raj, do you like Bangalore?'

'I love it. The weather is really awesome!'

'Have you made any friends yet?'

'Oh, I have lots of friends.'

'But you mentioned a best friend. You must be missing him.'

'Why would I? Bobby is here,' he replied.

That was interesting. The teenager had managed to find a best friend in such a short time. Was he someone who lived in the vicinity?

'What do you do together?'

'We only play video games in my room. Bobby doesn't like the boys here and tells me not to play with them.'

'Why doesn't Bobby like the boys?'

'He says they are very mean to him. They don't understand his accent and make fun of it.'

'Accent?' Aditya was surprised, 'Where's Bobby from?'

'He's come from London.'

'Does he have family in Bangalore?'

Raj shook his head.

'No, he stays with me at home here.'

Aditya wondered how Bobby's parents had allowed him to travel so far and for so long.

'Is Bobby Indian?' he asked.

'No, he's a Brit.'

'Isn't he missing school while he is here?'

'No, Bobby didn't go to a regular school in London. So it's okay.'

That sounded odd. Before Aditya could ask any more questions, Raj abruptly stood up.

'I have to go to my room now.' He mumbled something that sounded like, 'He's alone.'

Aditya saw the boy go and resumed reading the newspaper inattentively. Something was amiss but he couldn't quite put his finger on it.

Soon, Prakash returned from the shop. Deepa came at the same time with the tea.

'Now, that is good timing!' Prakash handed over the *samosas* and *jalebis* to Deepa and said, 'I've bought some chocolate for Raj. I'll give it to him and be back in a minute.'

Deepa poured out the tea in two cups.

'Sugar?'

'One, please.'

She stirred in a spoonful of sugar and handed Aditya a cup.

'Thanks.' He took a sip and casually asked, 'Who's Bobby?'

It was a simple question, but it startled Deepa and her face paled. In a split second things fell into place in Aditya's mind. He placed the cup on the coffee table and looked straight at Deepa. In a firm voice, he asked:

'Is there really a boy called Bobby? Has he come from London to be with Raj?'

Deepa looked down at the floor. Very slowly, she shook her head.

Aditya took a long breath. His suspicion was right – there was no Bobby; he was simply Raj's imaginary friend who had stepped out from the world of make believe to create havoc in their real lives. This was already serious. But Aditya needed to probe further to make the correct diagnosis.

'Deepa,' Aditya's voice was gentle. 'Please come to my clinic tomorrow.'

'Why?' Her voice was confrontational all over again.

'I can't talk to you in detail right now. I think Raj needs help. Prakash feels the same way too.'

She said vehemently, 'No, there's nothing wrong with Raj. It's just a phase. Children have imaginary friends. It will go away.'

'I know that smaller children make up stories, but he's a teenager now. Raj has crossed the age where a child believes in the existence of imaginary characters. I need to know why he still weaves such narratives. Please come tomorrow, Deepa.'

'I can't,' she refused without a second thought.

'Why? Don't you want your son to have a better life?'

'What better life did Naren have?' she was again agitated.

Why did she bring up Naren? Aditya was curious, but this wasn't the right time.

'Here's my card. It has my clinic's address. Can you come at 9 a.m. tomorrow?' Aditya asked in a firm voice.

'I'm still new to Bangalore. The roads are unfamiliar. I am not used to the bus and auto here. How will I come?' Her anger gave way to fatigue.

Prakash was standing near the door listening to the conversation.

'I'll take you,' he said softly.

Deepa turned towards him.

'But you are leaving tomorrow.'

'My train is in the evening. I'll take you to Aditya's clinic in the morning and I'll come back an hour later to pick you up.'

'I'll see you tomorrow then?' Aditya asked.

Deepa looked away.

***

Aditya was waiting the next morning when Deepa walked into his clinic on time. She was dressed as before in a nondescript *salwar-kameez* with a *dupatta* carelessly wrapped around her like a shawl. She looked haggard.

'Come into my room, Deepa.' Aditya held his room door open. As she stepped in, he pulled a chair out for her.

'Please sit down.'

'Thanks,' Deepa murmured.

Aditya moved to his own chair and waited for her to say something. She sat there without saying a word. Coming to a psychiatrist's clinic, to open up what she had kept to herself for years, was perhaps overwhelming. He offered her a glass of water.

'Tell me everything from the beginning. Just the way it happened. Please don't hold back,' he said.

'What do you want to know?' she asked him.

'Why don't we talk about Raj's childhood? Did you notice anything out of the ordinary – something that made you concerned?'

'No. He was all that a mother would ever want – very loving, obedient and happy. The sudden loss of his father must be the cause of his frustration and anger.'

'Was he very close to his father?'

She hesitated, 'He never expressed it, but I'm sure the attachment was deep.'

'Were his changes sudden? Did they happen soon after his father's death?' Aditya probed.

'Actually, no. I noticed them almost after a year. '

'What really happened to Naren?'

'I've told you already. It was an accident. He was going to work. As he was waiting at the station, he became unsteady and fell onto the tracks – right in front of an oncoming train.' Deepa repeated the same words that she had said the day before and in the same rehearsed manner.

Aditya let it go.

'How did you find out about Bobby?'

'Quite by chance.'

'Tell me more.'

Taking a deep breath she carefully chose her words.

'Like I told you earlier, I hadn't ever noticed anything unnatural about Raj – he was outgoing, a good student and a decent tennis player. He was very popular with his friends. But within a few months of Naren's death, he started changing. Usually, I returned home late from work. He was past the babysitter phase and was comfortable being on his own. Suddenly, I realised that he was scared to be by himself. Later, I found out that in my absence, he'd shut himself up in his room and lie in bed all the time. He didn't play or study until I returned. Obviously, his grades dipped. At first, I thought that he was unable to cope with his father's loss and at times, I suspected that he might even be doing drugs.'

'Drugs?'

Deepa nodded.

'Well, you hear horrible stories about teenagers in London and I didn't want to take any chances. One day, when Raj was in school, I stayed back at home and searched his room – closets, drawers and boxes. But I didn't find any drugs. Then I found something under his mattress – not really a diary, but a few pieces of paper held together by a big paper clip.'

'What did they say?'

'It was all about Bobby – what he did, what he said. That moment I grasped that there was an imaginary friend whose voice Raj heard constantly… Do you think he was hallucinating?'

'Could be,' Aditya was matter of fact.

'I think that it's more like a colourful imagination than hallucination. Raj was stressed out in London, with the pressures of a private school and the tennis practice on the weekends. Then there was the trauma of losing his father at such a young age. It's quite obvious that he wanted to escape to a make-believe world.' Deepa was talking to herself. It was a shallow explanation, but it was clear that she wanted to believe it.

'But his state still continues,' Aditya reminded her.

'I know, but it'll probably fade. The pressure in Bangalore is different. The teachers here have other expectations and there is this language issue. Students in his school don't follow his British accent and make fun of it. But Raj is a smart boy; he will adjust. We just need to be a little more patient. There's nothing to worry about,' she babbled on nervously. 'Just think about the cartoon character Calvin. His friend Hobbes is a stuffed tiger and Calvin has regular conversations with him. It's all imaginary. Maybe it's not hallucination at all!'

'That is a comic strip, Deepa. Even Calvin is imaginary. You know that,' Aditya said. 'It's true that hallucination involves sensing, seeing or even hearing things that aren't really there. Sometimes, it can be due to temporary physical factors or drug abuse, but frequently, it is a symptom of a mental disorder. We can't rule out that possibility yet.'

'No, that's not true! Raj doesn't have a mental disorder.'

'I'm not making a diagnosis yet, Deepa. I can't reach any conclusion with the little that I've learnt. Why don't you tell me what happened in school after your finding out about Bobby?'

Deepa struggled to keep her emotions in check before she spoke again.

'The school refused to keep him. So I transferred him to another school. But I started getting complaints from that school too. When I confronted Raj, he was shocked. He said, "I haven't done anything, Mama. It was Bobby. He does everything and now I get the blame."' Her voice choked as she continued, 'One day, Raj got upset for something very silly and broke the glasses at home right in front of me. When I asked him why he did that, his voice changed and he pleaded with me, "I haven't done anything, Bobby did that. When he gets angry, he breaks things. Mama, throw Bobby out of the house. Please, Mama."'

Deepa couldn't control herself anymore. Tears streamed down her face.

'I didn't know what to say to him. Tell me, Aditya, how do I get rid of someone who doesn't exist?'

Tough question. Tough situation. The prognosis was getting clearer. Raj's condition was not a temporary setback because of stress. It was much more serious. But Aditya didn't want to give any advice without absolute confirmation.

He glanced at the clock. An hour had already passed. His next patient was probably waiting outside. They'd have to continue at their next session.

'Deepa, do you have Raj's papers with you somewhere?'

She wiped her tears.

'Yes.'

'May I see them tomorrow?'

'I will send them across.'

'No, I want you to come here,' Aditya said. 'There may be some more details that you can fill me in on.'

'But Prakash is leaving tonight.'

'Now that you know where my clinic is, do you really need Prakash?'

She fidgeted.

'It's important, Deepa. Please come at 3 p.m.' Aditya needed to know more about her husband to discover the missing pieces of the jigsaw puzzle.

Deepa nodded feebly as she stood up to say goodbye.

6

The next day, Deepa showed up at the clinic at three. However, Aditya sensed a certain discomfort in her. She had gone into her shell; she was not going to talk about her past with anyone today.

'I thought I would be late. Not a single auto driver was willing to come this side. Finally, one driver agreed if I gave him triple the fare. Can you imagine?'

'What did you do?' Aditya went along with her.

'I had a travel agency's phone number. So I called them and hired a cab. I thought I might combine a few other errands as well.'

'Good thinking!'

'Cabs are expensive, but they're better when I have to run errands. Auto-rickshaws are horrendous on these pot-holed and busy roads,' she continued her inane conversation that stretched on to the weather, the infrastructure and the nuisance of cattle on the road. Eventually, she ran out of things and paused.

Seizing the opportunity, Aditya shifted the conversation.

'Deepa, have you brought Raj's papers?'

'No,' she replied. She was not looking forward to this conversation.

'Why is that?'

'I'm not sure if they'll be helpful.'

'Still, I'd like to have a look.' Aditya tried to be patient.

Deepa was strangely sullen. She didn't reply.

'Why don't you tell me more about Naren?' Aditya asked.

'Why do you always ask me about Naren? How is that important?' She sounded resentful.

'It's important for me to know, Deepa. Sometimes, there may be a genetic link. I'm asking you as a doctor.'

Deepa did not want to talk about her late husband; she wasn't going to come clean about him right now.

'If you must know, Naren was not an ideal man. He had his imperfections and lived in a bubble. He managed as best as he could and passed away in his mid-forties.'

Both of them remained silent for a while.

'I really need to see Raj's papers,' Aditya repeated.

This time Deepa conceded.

'Fine, I'll send them.'

'Why don't you bring Raj here next week? It's essential for me to talk to him before reaching any conclusion.'

'That's impossible! He won't agree to visit a psychiatrist's clinic; he'll definitely throw a tantrum.'

'Maybe he will, maybe he won't. You can present it nicely to him. After all, we had a pleasant conversation when we first met.'

'But I've told you all you wanted to know. Why do you want to meet him again? Isn't this a simple case of childhood trauma?'

'I can't say that yet, Deepa. I told you yesterday that I need to rule out the possibility of a mental illness.'

'Why do you keep repeating those words?' She was livid. 'I'm sorry to say this, but like most psychiatrists, you see a problem where there is none. Raj has no mental illness, Aditya. If you don't mind, I'll take your leave now; there's nothing else to discuss anyway. Thank you for your time.'

Suddenly, there was a loud crash in the reception. It startled both of them.

Aditya heard someone swearing followed by Aruna's irate protest. He rushed outside, while an inquisitive Deepa peeped to see what was happening.

There was complete mayhem in the reception area. The room looked like it had been hit by a tornado. The coffee table and the four cushioned chairs meant for visitors were pushed to one corner of the room. Aruna's desk was overturned; papers and files were strewn all over the floor. Four rowdy young men surrounded the pint-sized but angry Aruna. She stood her guard, hands on her hips, refusing to back down.

'Didn't you hear me?' she was screaming at them. 'Get out right now or I'm going to call the police.'

The leader of the group – a young man in a tight yellow t-shirt and faded jeans, a long line of vermillion drawn on his forehead, took threatening steps towards Aruna.

'Do you really think that we are scared of the bloody police?'

'Why don't we test that out?' Aruna said sarcastically as she picked up the telephone from the floor and started dialling.

The man in the yellow t-shirt shoved her aside and shouted:

'You bloody bitch! Don't even try that.'

'Mind your language, scoundrel, and keep your hands to yourself.' Aruna picked up a heavy paperweight and aimed it at him.

Before she could assault the man, another young man with embroidered jeans and a sleeveless black vest intervened. He placed a placating hand on the man in the yellow t-shirt and spoke to Aruna in a conciliatory tone:

'Madam, we aren't here to create any problems for anyone. We want to talk to the doctor for a few minutes and then I promise you that we'll leave.'

'After all this, how do you have the cheek to say that you don't intend to create any problem? What do you think you've done just now?'

'Okay, sorry, Madam, but Satish is really stressed about his mother.' He gestured to his two other cronies to pick up the papers from the floor and straighten the furniture. 'Can we see the doctor now?'

'Didn't I tell you already that the doctor is busy this evening? You can take an appointment to meet him at a later date.'

Aditya stared at Aruna in amazement. Anyone in her place would have been shaken by now. But not her. She hadn't even flinched. Aruna had grown up in a slum and was not a stranger to tough, male behaviour. In her twenty-nine years, she had had enough experience with crude men using foul language and violence. It was amazing how she had managed to educate herself, learnt to fight back. She was not afraid.

Satish marched towards her. The long scar on his right cheek – probably a nasty knife wound that had not been stitched up properly – looked hideous.

'Do you think that this is my first visit here? The doctor has seen my mother before and he gave her medicines that made her sick. That's why we are here. What do you think – we are here for something else?'

'Shut up, Satish.' Again, the man in the embroidered jeans butted in. 'Madam, his mother needs treatment. We'll only take a few minutes of the doctor's time.'

It was then that Aditya heard whimpering and noticed a fifth figure crouching on the floor. It was an old woman and she was looking dazed. Probably Satish's mother.

'Leave me. Please leave me alone, and let me go home,' she started pleading with her son.

'Stop whining!' Satish snarled at the old woman. She recoiled and started moaning again.

Aditya stepped forward to look at the old woman; she looked familiar. Had he seen her before?

He turned to Aruna.

'What's going on here?'

Aruna was visibly relieved to see Aditya.

'Sir, these ruffians didn't call before coming. They just barged in and demanded to see you. When I told them that it is not possible today, they started threatening me.'

Aditya confronted the group.

'What do you want?'

'Ah, there you are, Doctor.' Satish walked up to him. 'Didn't I tell you not to give my mother any medicine? But you ignored me completely. Now see what's happened.'

Then it all came back to Aditya. It was now his turn to be angry.

'How dare you come here again? Leave right now.'

'Give us the right medicine and we'll leave.'

'Medicine for what?' Aditya snapped at him.

'Don't try to act smart. I am not foolish enough to believe you like my father. You gave my mother some wrong medicine and she's gotten worse. Now change all that.'

'You are wasting my time. Your mother was unwell when she came to me. Now she is back to normal with the medicines and you should be grateful. Take her back.'

'But there was nothing wrong with her in the first place,' Satish pressed on.

'When your father brought her to me three years ago, she was a wreck.'

'What does he mean?' Satish turned towards his friend and asked.

'The doctor is saying that your mother was mad,' the friend clarified.

'What?' Satish was enraged. 'If my mother was mad, then how could she forecast the future of all her devotees? You are a fraud. I am warning you one last time. Make her like she was before.'

'What do you mean – make her like before?'

'The way she was before my father brought her to you.'

'You mean you want me to turn her back into Lord Shiva's sidekick? That isn't possible anymore. At least, I can't do that. But you can try and pray. Maybe God will grant you your wish.' Aditya could not help being disdainful.

Satish's fists tightened and his eyes turned red. He was shaking in anger.

'How dare you? How can you make fun of God? Your family will die and you'll have the most painful death ever. People will spit at you…'

Two policemen walked in, ending the conversation. Obviously, Aruna had called them from her cell phone. Satish was bundled off into the police van. Within minutes, all his cronies changed their tune and offered to take the old woman back to the village.

Aditya walked back into the room and apologised to Deepa.

'I'm sorry for walking out in the middle of our session.'

'What was all that about?' Deepa had forgotten her problems for now.

'Did you see the whimpering old woman? I had treated her once. It took some time but she eventually became normal. Now, the son wants her illness back.'

Deepa looked puzzled.

'Why would anyone want that?'

'The thing is… the old woman was convinced that she was Lord Shiva's assistant.'

'She thought she was a God-woman?'

'Actually, in the beginning the old lady never made such a proclamation. Her son drilled the idea into her head and conned simple villagers into believing that his mother was the Chosen One.'

'Chosen for what?'

'It is a long story,' Aditya said quietly.

'Tell me,' she said.

'Three years ago on a day like this, there was a commotion in the office. I stepped out of my room into the reception and found this same old woman sitting on top of the receptionist's table.'

'What did Aruna do? I really admire the way she handled those men today.'

'Aruna was not working for me then. I had a timid girl, Nalini, as my receptionist and the poor thing was crouching near the door trembling with fright.'

'But the old woman looks so harmless!'

'Not that day. She was wearing a bright red silk sari with a golden border and her hair was loose, her face was flushed. There was a huge red *bindi* on her forehead and her kohl-rimmed eyes were wild. She looked like the reincarnation of the Goddess Kali and was rambling like an oracle, swaying to and fro in a hypnotic manner. Every now and then, she would let out a horrendous blood-curdling scream.'

'That must have been scary.'

'It was more irritating than scary. At first, I thought that the old woman and her husband had come to extract money, but when he pleaded with me to have a look at her, I could not stay angry and agreed to hear them out. Apparently, the old woman had gone into a trance a few weeks ago and after that, she had started mumbling odd things. Their son took advantage of the situation and spread the word that a Goddess had entered his mother's body and that she could predict the future.'

'But how could her predictions come true?'

'Well, some simple and silly ones came true, while Satish and his group interpreted the rest in such a manner that it all sounded believable. The villagers were impressed and Satish began to make a lot of money. However, the old man realised that all was not well with his wife and asked around. Someone recommended me to him and he came here. I treated the old woman and she started responding quite well for a year until Satish one day barged into my office while I was seeing his parents. He and his cronies dragged the parents out and that was the last time I saw them. Until today.'

'But why were they back?' Deepa was perplexed.

'I don't know but my guess is that the old woman must have continued her medications. Her illness is probably now under control. That means that she is no longer an oracle and the son can no longer earn money from her illness. That's why he's furious.'

'What illness did the old woman have?'

'She had what we call possession syndrome disorder. It is quite common in our culture.'

'What is that?'

'You must have seen people getting possessed – supposedly by some God. This woman used to think that she was Ma Chamunda… She was obviously hallucinating.'

Deepa was inquisitive.

'Does one hallucinate because of this possession syndrome?'

'No, there can be many other reasons. Sometimes one hallucinates because of a chemical imbalance in the brain.'

'Why does a chemical imbalance happen?'

'It can be due to DNA, sometimes drugs; there could be many reasons.'

She listened intently.

'Does Raj have something like that?'

'I cannot tell off hand. Each case is unique; we cannot compare one with another.'

'Is it something dangerous?' She was talking about her son.

'It could be,' he replied carefully. 'In most cases, auditory and visual hallucinations are accepted as a symptom of schizophrenia.'

There was terror in Deepa's eyes. In a barely audible voice, she mumbled, 'Aditya, my husband Naren... he... he had schizophrenia.'

Aditya was speechless.

It was true that he had suspected her son's disorder as genetic, but he had not foreseen such a direct connection.

'Now you must realise how important it is for me to meet Raj,' he said.

Deepa nodded.

'I'll discuss it with him and try to get him here.'

7

An entire week went by, but Deepa did not call. Finally she did on a day when Aditya's cell phone was on silent mode, and he was in the middle of an appointment, listening to one of the most harrowing and heart-breaking tales he had ever heard.

***

The lady before Aditya, whose name was Shabnam, was referred by Dr Jonathan Das. Jonathan was the founder of a non-profit organisation and over time, Aditya and he had become close friends. He regularly sent poor people with possible mental disorders to Aditya for free treatment. But Shabnam wasn't the usual referral – she was from a middle-class family.

When she walked into Aditya's office, Shabnam's courage and words suddenly failed her. It was nothing unusual for Aditya; the first meeting with a psychiatrist was typically always stressful.

He spoke in a kind voice:

'Shabnam, Jonathan said that you wanted to meet a psychiatrist and that something was bothering you.'

She nodded.

'Please tell me about it.'

There was silence. She stared at the floor.

'What is troubling you, Shabnam?'

'I have a problem,' she said, still looking down.

'What problem do you have?'

'No, no, not me,' she was flustered.

'Then who?'

She didn't respond.

'Jonathan told me that you had visited a gynaecologist a few days earlier.'

Shabnam nodded again.

'May I see the prescription?' asked Aditya.

She opened her black purse and fished out a folded piece of paper. Reluctantly, she handed it over to Aditya.

The prescription was from Dr Jayita Somasekhar. Aditya skimmed over it and found what he was looking for – gonorrhoea! Poor thing!

'Don't make any judgements about me,' Shabnam straightened her back and said fiercely, before he could ask anything further.

'Why would I do that?' Aditya asked, astonished by her forcefulness.

'Everyone does. When I first went to a doctor near my house, he behaved as if I had come straight from the red-light area. Later, Dr Jonathan sent me to Dr Jayita, but she was terribly harsh with me and behaved like it was my fault.'

Aditya pursed his lips. He did not know Jayita Somasekhar personally, but he had heard about her high-handed ways from other doctors; the woman was known to be efficient, but extremely rude. He made a mental note to tell Jonathan not to send any patient to that woman again.

'So you contracted this disease from your husband?' he asked Shabnam.

She lowered her head.

'Be frank with me. Otherwise, how can I help you?'

At last, she looked up at him.

Aditya was gentle.

'Tell me about yourself. Where do you stay?'

'I live near the big Hanuman temple.'

'Do you work?'

'No, I studied only till the tenth grade. I could not finish school because my parents got me married young.'

'How old were you at the time of your wedding?'

'Fifteen.'

'Fifteen! Didn't your parents know that it is illegal for a girl to get married before the age of eighteen?'

'They knew it, but...' her voice trailed off.

It was fruitless. Yes, it was illegal but how many people in the country respect the law? Even their maid Lakshmi had married off her fourteen-year-old daughter only recently. When Aditya and Prachi tried to explain the legal implications, Lakshmi had nonchalantly remarked:

'That law is only for the rich. It isn't practical for us. We live in a slum; there are all kinds of bad people moving about freely. How else do I keep my girl safe other than getting her married as soon as I can?'

But Shabnam's situation was different; she wasn't from a poor family. Aditya wondered why her parents got her married at fifteen. But then, in India every community has their own rules and traditions.

He sighed and let it go.

'You could have finished school after your marriage. Why didn't you? Did your in-laws oppose your studying further?'

'No, not that. My in-laws are the nicest people in the world. But…' she hesitated. 'I became pregnant.'

Things were a little muddled here.

'Look, Shabnam,' Aditya said, 'there's something you aren't telling me. I need to know everything there is to know.'

Shabnam looked at the door, almost like she wanted to flee. But in an instant, she steeled herself and in a barely audible voice, she explained.

'He was my brother's friend and visited our house often when my brother was around. Later, he deliberately started coming over when I was the only one at home. He used to bring all kinds of magazines and show me obscene pictures. One time, I just lost my head… I became pregnant. Then they coerced us to get married.'

'Who did?'

There were tears in her eyes.

'My parents.My in-laws.The community elders.'

'Tell me about your husband. How was it when both of you got married?'

Shabnam shrugged.

'Average, I guess. Not good. Not bad. We were living in a joint family and life was manageable. Physically, he demanded a lot.'

Aditya understood that she was referring to sex.

'But I was young and healthy and I didn't have an aversion to it,' she continued.

'How long did it last?'

'For a while. It remained even after my older son was born. But when I became pregnant with my second child, he became less demanding.'

'Didn't that make you suspicious?'

'No. I thought that fatherhood had made him more responsible. But I was wrong.'

'Why do you say that?'

'Once, I caught him exposing himself and showing pornographic magazines to his niece – his own sister's daughter. I wanted to leave him right then. But where would I go? My father was dead and my mother had moved to Kanpur to live with my brother. I didn't have money to move out on my own.

So I stayed. I tried to warn my sister-in-law, but her daughter refused to corroborate what had happened. Maybe she was scared… I tried to tell myself that maybe I was wrong. Maybe I had just misunderstood the situation.'

Shabnam took a deep breath and continued.

'A few months later, he did the same to a girl from our neighbourhood. Unlike his niece, that girl created a furore and he was caught. The neighbours thrashed him and made it impossible for him to live in the area. We had to leave his parents' house and moved into a rented home elsewhere.'

'Didn't your in-laws counsel him?'

'Of course they did. But he wasn't willing to listen to anybody. He started visiting prostitutes after that.'

'Your sons are adults now. What do they think of their father?'

'My younger son was a good student. Somehow, my brother-in-law managed to get him admission in a military school and my son went to live in a hostel even though he was very young. He has a good job now and regularly sends me money, but he never comes home. I think he knows about his father.'

'What about your older son?'

'My older son isn't intelligent. I don't think he ever realised his father's habits. He is married now and adores his new wife and is protective about her.'

Aditya had a feeling he knew what was coming.

Shabnam was uneasy and spoke haltingly.

'I don't know how to tell you this; my husband is such a lecherous man that he has started preying upon our daughter-in-law. I've ensured that nothing untoward happened so far, but instinctively I know that the girl is uncomfortable. I can't leave my daughter-in-law alone at home, even for a minute. Today, I left her at her uncle's house on my way here and I will pick her up on my way back. But how long can I do this? I'm so scared… one misstep can lead to something terrible…'

For a moment, Aditya lost his clinical guard and his heart went out to the woman.

'Dr Das told me that my husband can be treated, but only by a psychiatrist. That's why I've come here.'

'You are right. There is a condition called hypersexuality. It sounds like that is the case here; it is a mental illness.'

Shabnam broke down.

'Just tell me the truth, Doctor. Is there a way out?'

'Yes, it can be treated. Bring your husband to me. After I see him, I will get an MRI done. It can help us some. Once it is confirmed, the treatment can start.'

'But how will I make him come to you?' There was helplessness in her voice. 'He will skin me alive if he even knew that I was here.'

'You can force him to come by letting him know about the gonorrhoea. You can also threaten him with a possible police complaint.'

'I'll try,' she said, unhappy at the thought of confronting her husband. 'Maybe this is my *taqdir*. My destiny. I must have done something awful to be saddled with a lewd man like him.'

'Don't hold yourself responsible. Once I talk to your husband and run a few tests, we can take this further,' Aditya added.

'Will he become all right after that?'

'I can't tell you anything at this time. I need to see him and talk to him. But I can tell you this – he will have to go for psychotherapy.'

'Psychotherapy? What's that?'

'When your husband goes for therapy, he'll be able to talk to a trained professional who is called a therapist. From that conversation, the therapist will understand why he does what he does.'

'My in-laws talked to him regularly. They've tried their best to change his attitude, but nothing worked. Why will this work?'

'His parents are close to him and it is impossible for them to have an objective conversation. A therapist will do the job dispassionately. They are trained to do this. It is easier for someone to open up with a therapist once a relationship is in place.'

Shabnam was quiet for a few minutes as she tried to absorb the information. When she finally stood up to leave, there was a glint of hope in her eyes.

'I'll try. I'll definitely try to bring my husband here.'

***

When Shabnam left, Aditya glanced at his cell phone and saw Deepa's missed call. He took a few moments to gather his thoughts and called her back.

'Sorry, I missed your call earlier. I was in a session,' he said.

'That's okay. I thought as much.' She went straight to the point, 'Aditya, I talked to Raj and he has agreed to come and see you. He thinks that maybe his friend Bobby is the one who needs to see you.'

'It doesn't matter. Let him think that way. Will you come tomorrow?' Aditya checked his calendar as he spoke.

'No, tomorrow won't work. I'm going to Trivandrum with Raj. Naren's parents are conducting an elaborate *puja* for his death anniversary on Friday. They do it every year and I have never been able to attend. Now that I am in India with Raj, I think I should.'

'Yes, that's a good idea.'

'I will be back next Monday and Raj and I can come to your clinic on Tuesday. Will that be okay?'

'That's fine, Deepa. I'll see you on Tuesday then.'

'But wait, Aditya,' she stopped him before he could hang up. 'Can I meet you today for a few minutes?'

'Sure. Come anytime after 2 p.m. I am free till three.'

'I want to give you something,' she added.

'Oh yes! The papers that Raj has written about Bobby?'

'That, too.' She paused. 'There's something else. I'll see you at two.'

8

When Deepa entered Aditya's office in the afternoon, she hesitated to sit down. She was very nervous and kept fidgeting.

'Have you brought the papers?' Aditya asked.

'Yes.' She opened the bag and handed him a transparent file containing a sheaf of papers.

'Why don't you take a seat?'

'No, I have to go. But… but I want you to read this.' She took out a hardbound volume that looked like a diary.

'Is that also Raj's diary?'

'No. It's my journal.'

When Aditya had first met Deepa, he was amused that she maintained a journal. She refused to call it a diary. One day when they were alone, he had asked her, 'Why do you call it a journal? Why not call it a diary?'

'Diaries are just an account of events, but journals reflect people's innermost thoughts and feelings about things that have happened.'

'Will you let me read it?' he had asked her somewhat playfully.

'No. It's personal,' she had replied seriously.

In a quick moment, Aditya collected himself. He chided the voice within for distracting him.

'You wanted to know all about Naren, didn't you? Well, this journal will tell you everything. I started writing it soon after my marriage and I continued writing it till the day he died. I wasn't regular; I only wrote when things became unmanageable. But you'll get some insight about Naren and my life from it. Maybe it'll help you understand Raj better.'

'Thanks, Deepa.'

'See you on Tuesday. Bye.' She turned to leave, but stopped near the door. Aditya sensed that something was still bothering her.

She walked back to him, gave him a half-smile and said:

'Aditya, I have another journal that I wrote after Naren's death. That will tell you the timeline and sequence of events leading up to Raj's symptoms.' She took out another hardbound notebook from her bag. Her right hand was trembling and her face was flushed.

'I'll be careful with your journals, Deepa. Nobody but me will have access to them.'

'I know that… Bye.'

She walked out of the door.

The moment Deepa left, Aditya took out Raj's papers from the transparent file. The first page was a cover with 'Bobby', written on it colourfully.

Aditya started reading. Each page had just a paragraph or two, but the words reflected a very disturbed mind. At Raj's age, the world should have been a magical place, but it was filled with disillusionment and frustration. The chronicle was in Bobby's voice: the dark, gloomy thoughts portrayed in it were supposed to be Bobby's.

After browsing through the pages, Aditya put the file away. He looked at Deepa's journals, wishing he had time to go through them right away; the answer to the mystery of a genetic link was in there. But it was already 3 p.m. and time for his next appointment.

The rest of the afternoon was a blur with one patient after another.

***

At the end of the day, Aditya took the journals home, hoping to work on them in his study, but it never happened. When he reached home, he discovered that Prachi's second cousin Jayant had invaded the place with his loudmouth wife Smita and their spoilt son Litu. Jayant, who lived in Ramanagara, a town not far away from Bangalore, had arrived, as always, without giving any prior notice.

'What a surprise, Jayant!' Aditya tried his best to curb the irritation. 'You should have called me before coming. I would have picked up some chocolates for Litu.'

'That's okay. You can buy them tomorrow,' Jayant replied casually.

'What brings you to Bangalore?'

'I have some work at the Indian Institute of Science for two days and then it's the weekend, anyway. So all of us thought of coming here.'

'That's nice. It is a great idea to have a short vacation.' The sarcasm in Aditya's voice did not even touch Jayant.

'I wish we could stay longer.' Aditya's intent was lost on him. 'But Smita's parents are arriving from Kolkata on Sunday morning. We'll pick them up from Bangalore Railway Station and then go back home... Prachi, where is the tea?'

'Here you go.' Prachi walked in with tea and biscuits. Aditya noticed that she looked tired and was still in the sari that she wore in the morning. Obviously, she had not had the chance to change. This family was such a pest.

'Why didn't you give a call before coming, Jayant? What if Prachi and I were away?'

'Where would you go this time of the year? It's not easy for doctors like you to stay away from your patients. Anyway, had you both not been around, I would have gone to Smita's uncle's house in Hosur.'

Smita joined in.

'He lives in a joint family and it is not easy for us to be with so many people, but at least they always welcome us into their home. So see, we did have a back-up plan.'

Jayant nodded and reached for a biscuit.

Prachi and Aditya exchanged a swift glance of despair.

'Hey, Prachi, these biscuits are like sawdust. Both of you are really so health-conscious. Make something more interesting – maybe spicy hot *pakodas*? I'll have another cup of tea as well. Please add more sugar in my cup. God, I'm so hungry!' Jayant reached out for another biscuit despite his complaint.

'Did you show your report to Aditya?' Smita suddenly asked her husband.

'Not yet,' he replied.

Aditya was curious.

'What report?'

'Just some blood work. My cholesterol is really high. Can we do something about that?' Jayant asked between bites of another biscuit.

Sure. Keep eating biscuits and ask for more *pakodas* and fried food. But don't stop there. While you are at it, splurge on pastries and sweets. You are only ninety kilograms right now. Why don't you aim for a full century? Aditya was furious inside. Who wanted to be with two uncouth adults and their wild child? What really disappointed him was the fact that now he wouldn't be able to touch Deepa's journal for three whole days. Friday and Saturday were busy days in the clinic anyway and Aditya would not have time to go over her journals in detail.

After three horrendous days, Jayant and his family finally said good-bye to their harried hosts on Sunday morning after a sumptuous brunch. As the cab took the family away, both Prachi and Aditya heaved a sigh of relief. Prachi ran up the stairs into their bedroom to sleep. Aditya shut himself in his study and took out Deepa's journal.

***

It was a blue-bound notebook, the cover had birds flying into the sunset. He turned to the first page. It was penned the same day that Deepa's note had reached him soon after the wedding date was finalised.

Deepa wrote: *It is over and done with. Today I broke up with the one person who was my true love and with whom I had dreamt of spending the rest of my life. I cannot blame anyone else other than myself for this misery. If I let myself fall in love, then I should have had the courage to stand up to the commitment. I could not. I could not defy my family, the societal norms, and the century-long traditions. Why couldn't I rebel? Why did I give in so meekly? What right did I have to fall in love and bring misery to another human being?*

Aditya stopped reading. As a psychiatrist, it was important for him to know the facts and a description of Naren's illness, but now he felt like a voyeur. He pulled out of it and the psychiatrist in him managed to win.

Slowly, he turned the page.

9

Deepa was seventeen at the time of her engagement with Naren. In her community, it was the done thing and Deepa did not have much say in the matter. She was grateful that at least her parents had let her meet and talk to the prospective groom a couple of times, though it was always with someone around. She knew that Naren was brilliant and from a good family, but she did not feel an instant attraction to the man. Maybe that would happen after marriage, maybe this was how it was, she tried to tell herself.

Her marriage was to take place six months after, but all of a sudden, Naren changed his mind. He wanted more time. He wanted to finish his doctorate, which was still three years away, before tying the knot. The families from both sides were not happy about this decision, but Deepa was relieved. She looked at it as an opportunity to know her fiancé better and probably, time would make her heart fonder. But that never really happened. Naren did not try to contact her after their engagement. Even when Deepa sent him a card on his birthday with a short note, he didn't acknowledge it. She felt humiliated, but told herself that probably Naren was old-fashioned.

That was the time around when she met her cousin Prakash for the first time and with him, Aditya.

She had nothing much in common with Aditya – a medical student, who was from another state and a different culture, but there was an inexplicable attraction. Deepa fell in love with him. She was a traditional girl brought up in a conservative family and knew that as a betrothed, she wasn't supposed to be attracted to another person, but she could not help herself. She had no idea where it would all lead to and naïvely she thought that somehow things would sort themselves out. But, of course, they didn't. Deepa had to comply with her parent's wishes and marry Naren.

The wedding ceremony had hiccups. The glitches weren't because of the usual reasons that happen in arranged marriages; there was no dowry-related issue or dissatisfaction with the wedding arrangements by the family of the groom. The problem was the groom himself. Naren complained non-stop. He whined about the heat, the venue, the food and even the ceremony. Why wasn't the wedding arranged indoors in the comfort of air-conditioning? He rudely asked for the wedding ceremony to be shortened. The groom's family was embarrassed at his behaviour and unseemly demands and did not know how to go about it.

Thankfully, Deepa's family elders were gracious and had a conversation with the priests. The rituals ended soon after.

Naren's tantrum during the wedding shocked Deepa, and the next incident that happened later that night didn't help either. Deepa's idea about a wedding night was romantic. It came partly from giggly descriptions by her married girlfriends and partly from movies. But when Naren came into the room, he stared at her and said harshly, 'You have a big nose! How did I miss that during the times I saw you earlier?'

Deepa was taken aback and didn't know how to react.

'But wow, what a figure you have!' He grabbed her with urgency. Before she knew it, he had undressed both of them.

***

Soon after the wedding, Deepa left for London. It was her first time on a plane. She was excited and scared – not sure what the future held for her. Surprisingly, after the wedding and the first physical encounter, Naren came across differently. He was attentive, polite and charming. Deepa was amazed. Maybe it was the stress that had brought out the beast in him. Things would be fine from now, she thought, as they began their new life together.

The British Airways flight landed in London on a rare sunny afternoon and Deepa was enchanted with the wonderful city that seemed to welcome her. She soaked in the ambience during the hour-long taxi drive to Naren's home.

*****

Naren was eccentric, impulsive and absolutely useless at managing his life, but somehow, he had squirrelled away most of his money during his doctorate. Just before their marriage, he used the savings to make a down payment for a small cottage in the suburbs. The place was rundown with an unkempt garden, but it was home and Deepa fell in love with it.

Naren liked the way she went about tidying the house and the garden. One day he told her:

'We have to get you new clothes.'

'What clothes?'

'Some trousers, sweaters and skirts. You can't be going around London in your saris.'

Deepa went with him to the big department stores on Oxford Street. To Mark and Spencer, Debenhams and John Lewis. He chose the western dresses that she now must wear and Deepa let him.

Naren also took her to see Buckingham Palace, the Tower Bridge, Westminster Abbey, St Paul's Cathedral and the British Museum. Then there were trips to Southbank, Covent Garden, Trafalgar Square and Piccadilly Circus. Deepa gaped at the London Eye and couldn't get enough of the Thames. She had only read about these places in books and seen them in the movies. She was enchanted.

Amidst all this, there was just one incident that bothered her for quite a few days, but finally, she convinced herself that it wasn't anything big and she was reading too much meaning into a simple situation.

It all happened like this. They had just completed the Oxford University tour when Deepa saw her husband distracted – it was as if his eyes were searching for something.

'Are you looking for a Thai restaurant?' she asked playfully. In the past few weeks, she had realised that Naren loved Thai food and never missed a chance to have it.

'How did you know?' Naren's voice was hard.

'I know.' Deepa smiled.

'You can read my mind?'

'Maybe.' Her voice was as playful as before.

'How? Have you implanted something in my brain?'

'What!' Deepa was taken aback with Naren's misgivings. 'I was just joking. How could I do that?'

'Okay. Whatever.' Naren's voice sounded strange

Instinctively, Deepa suspected that it wasn't okay, but she let it go.

***

Deepa's next entry in the journal brought a smile to Aditya's lips. She had written, 'Oh my God, I cannot believe this! College! Naren wants me to do my under-graduation. I know it will probably not be Oxford, but how does it matter? Any reputed college in London is good. Oh my God! I still cannot believe that I will soon dive into the world of English language and literature. I want to dance. I want to hug Naren. I want to kiss him.'

Deepa got her admission though she hardly got any credit for the years in college in India. It did not matter to her; she was willing to start all over again. But amidst the excitement of her new start, what troubled her was the fact that she sometimes sensed Naren was not happy that she was going out of the home by herself. It was as if on the one hand, he wanted to give and on the other, wanted to take everything away. The contrasting emotions puzzled her.

One day, when Deepa was struggling with a paper on Chaucer, Naren came and sat down in the next chair.

'So tell me,' he asked, 'what all do you do in your college?'

'Don't ask. Sometimes the papers are so tough, I really get stressed out.'

'I am not asking about your studies. You know, with all the men and women together, there has to be something going on all the time.'

Deepa shrugged.

'Sure. That happens.'

'What about you?'

Naren's smirk irritated Deepa.

'What about me? The whole campus knows that I am married.'

'Since when has that been an impediment?'

Deepa ignored the jibe, but by the time she completed her studies, she realised that Naren's attitude towards her and anything connected to her had become unpredictable. He became irritable, moody and largely negative about everything. She didn't know how to deal with all this, hoping that it was transitory and would go away in time like before. It didn't. Instead, Naren became fidgety. The things that once made him happy, like the well-kept house, pretty garden, Deepa's grades, started exasperating him. He was also becoming somewhat suspicious and distrustful of his wife.

Deepa struggled until an ugly incident happened. It was after an office party. On the way home, in the taxi, Naren was sullen and remote, refusing even to look at his wife. The moment they entered the privacy of their home, he turned around and slapped her hard. 'Why were you flirting with Paul tonight? You don't have to seduce him for my promotion. I can take care of myself. Do you understand?' he screamed at a shocked and baffled Deepa, who did not even know how to react to such a vile accusation.

She was fearful, angry and sad. She retreated into a shell and as time passed, she became very reserved in the presence of any man. Still, it wasn't enough. Soon, she realised that Naren's jealousy was not directed only towards men; he disliked his wife having a friendly relationship with women as well. For the sake of her marriage, Deepa isolated herself from others. But he continued to be suspicious. Despite the reservations about his wife's fidelity, Naren's sexual drive remained unabated. She handled it just the way she was handling everything else – she accepted it and gave in whenever he demanded physical intimacy.

With the passage of time, the lonely and restrictive existence made her claustrophobic and sometimes, she felt like a cornered animal that wanted to escape, but her traditional upbringing restrained her. It was her destiny and she must learn to accept it.

Seven years after her marriage, their son came. Deepa hoped that the arrival of the baby would make things better. It did, somewhat, but its place was promptly filled with a shroud of unease.

The newborn had inherited his mother's complexion and beautiful eyes, but the broad forehead, sharp nose and dimpled cheeks were entirely Naren's. It was such a strong resemblance that even strangers remarked on it. But to Deepa's dismay, Naren seemed unsure. He never cuddled the baby. Frequently, he would check on his son's features.

One day, Deepa found him standing next to Raj's crib comparing him with his own childhood photograph. She was curious and asked him what the matter was. He turned to her and asked, 'Am I really his father?' At first, Deepa thought that he was joking and laughed it off, but then another time when Raj kept waking up through the night, Naren commented, 'My mother used to say I always slept through the night as a baby. Are you sure that this is my son?'

Increasingly, he started seeing dissimilarities. His conversations became derisive. After a few months, Deepa was so disgusted that she dragged him for a paternity test. The results clearly showed that he was the father, but even that did not end his doubts. He suspected the technician who performed the test and asked her at home, 'How much did you pay him for the test results?'

When Deepa didn't respond, he goaded her.

'You took care of him some other way?'

No more, she told herself as she swallowed the insult. She would not remain in this toxic environment any more. Deepa seriously considered a separation and thought about contacting a lawyer.

However, before anything could happen, something bizarre took place. One day, while the couple was shopping for groceries at their local store, Naren could not locate her in the aisles and got into a frenzy. His body became stiff, he blanked out and collapsed on the floor.

The store staff immediately summoned emergency services and Naren was rushed to a hospital nearby. The subsequent events devastated Deepa. Past medical records were unearthed. She was shocked to find out that Naren had been treated for schizophrenia before and had never told her about it. Deepa had no idea how to deal with this enormous problem. But one thing was sure. She wasn't going to abandon her husband in that condition.

She brought Naren back from the hospital and nursed him till he became his earlier self. But he wasn't cooperative when it came to his medication. Left with no other choice, Deepa started mixing it in his food. Once the medication kicked in, it brought forth a dramatic change in Naren. His mood swings lessened and there was hardly any trace of the earlier abusive behaviour.

One Friday morning, Deepa was in the process of mixing the medication into his porridge when Naren walked into the kitchen. She froze, but to her relief, he promised his wife that he would take care of himself and have his medicines regularly. She didn't have to mix them with his food anymore. He said he wanted them to be a normal family.

Deepa believed her husband; she desperately wanted to.

Meanwhile, Raj grew older and started school. His parents enrolled him in a private school. Naren's salary was enough to take care of the fees and other sundry school expenses but he was always very stingy. That was when Deepa thought about getting a job. As soon as she had a few offers in hand, she spoke to Naren.

To Deepa's surprise, he was supportive. She felt uneasy; she wasn't sure what was going on in her husband's mind. In a few weeks, her apprehension proved right. Naren retreated into his jealous self and started questioning her fidelity. His wife's status as a working woman gave him another channel for accusations. The toxic atmosphere at home was back and Deepa's life became miserable once again. One day, her patience almost snapped when she came home later than usual after an important meeting. She was hungry and tired. As she turned the key in the lock and pushed the door open, she saw Naren standing in front of her with a sneer.

'Are you tired?' he asked her.

'Yes, it was a long day.'

'Tell me something,' he dramatically lowered his voice and winked. 'How many did you romp today?'

***

Aditya closed his eyes for a few minutes; he could imagine the pain Deepa would have gone through. That particular day she was too exhausted and upset to react. But as she brushed past him to take a shower and change, she told herself this was it. It was not possible for her to continue living with Naren, illness or no illness. She would go to a divorce lawyer as soon as possible.

Deepa couldn't separate from her husband right away. She had a first meeting with a lawyer, but there was an extraordinary change in Naren before the second meeting. His awful accusations vanished. It was replaced by something else. He became aloof.

After the shopping aisle episode, the psychiatrist had sat her down to explain Naren's illness.

'The term schizophrenia is a combination of two words – *skhizein*, that is to split and *phren*, that is the mind,' he had said. 'But schizophrenia does not mean a split mind nor does it refer to a split personality. Several factors must be taken into consideration; sometimes, there are factors beyond our control. As a caregiver, you must be alert and consult a psychiatrist immediately if you notice anything out of the ordinary.'

But Deepa did not accurately understand the doctor. She should have consulted the psychiatrist when she saw Naren's aloof behaviour, but she didn't. She welcomed the calm, not realising what was soon to follow.

It all started when they ran into George at the tube station. They knew him through another friend. George looked very pulled down. Deepa was concerned and asked him if he had been unwell. George told her that he had unexpectedly lost his wife to leukaemia a month ago.

Before a shocked Deepa could even convey her condolences, Naren said, 'Good, good,' and laughed loudly. George walked away dismayed and hurt, but Deepa knew that something was very wrong with her husband. She dithered. Should she take him to the psychiatrist, or was the man just cruel? However, before she could even take a decision, his abusive behaviour returned with such a vengeance that Deepa had to call emergency services this time. Naren was forcefully taken to a psychiatric hospital.

The truth came out. The doctor said that Naren had stopped taking his medication a long time ago and his problem had intensified with the passage of time.

The schizophrenia had deteriorated and he would have to be hospitalised for some time.

The hospital stay lasted for almost two months. When Naren finally came home, the alarming change in him was both physical and mental. His body movements had slowed down and he often looked blank, but what really pained Deepa was his mental state. With all the strong medication that he was taking, Naren's mind wasn't his any more and most of the time he talked in a childish manner. He could not go to work. The doctor advised Deepa to fill his days with hobby-based activities.

She got Naren admission into a vocational training institute nearby where he was taught to print blocks on fabric. Deepa knew that the training would never give him a source of real income, but at least it kept him occupied.

Until one day.

It started on an innocuous note. Deepa sent Raj to school, helped Naren to get ready and they walked to the tube station. It was the rush hour and they missed the regular train by a few seconds. The next one was seven minutes away. Deepa sat down on a wooden bench while Naren paced back and forth in front of her. As soon as she saw the approaching train, and stood up to gather her things, she saw a huge commotion and realised that someone had jumped in front of the train. She looked around and suddenly felt her heart sink when she could not find Naren where he had been. She ran to where the crowd had already formed. The station police was trying to keep people at bay. Still, she managed to get a glimpse of the body that was lying on the tracks. It was mangled beyond recognition but then she saw the red jacket with the herringbone stripes. It was the one that Naren had insisted on wearing that morning.

***

The next entry in her journal began with a Jane Austen quote: 'I grieved because I could not grieve. There were no tears, just a strange sense of relief.' But this relief, a closure of sorts, made her feel petty and nasty. She suffered from a sense of guilt for weeks. Finally, one day, she managed to let it go.

Aditya re-read the last paragraph of the first journal meticulously. Deepa had written:

I should have been in India for Naren's memorial services and mourned his death with his family, but I decided not to go through with the sham. His parents understood, I'm sure, and they did not insist. I didn't share my pain in all these years, but they knew. They were grateful that I did not abandon their son in his illness. That chapter is closed now and there's nothing more to discuss. Something tells me that though I am stuck in a dark tunnel right now, I must keep walking ahead with confidence. There will be light at the end of the tunnel, with Ethan around.

***

Prachi peeped into his study. 'It is almost midnight, Aditya.'

Aditya yawned, 'Really? I didn't realise it was this late.'

'You look tired.'

'Why didn't you come by earlier?'

'You were engrossed in work and I didn't want to disturb you.'

'Thank God, I don't have any morning appointments. I can go a little late to the clinic tomorrow. Come, let's go to bed.'

Aditya switched off the lights and followed her to their bedroom.

10

Aditya had wanted to sleep late. But his body was so accustomed to waking up early at a particular time that he was wide awake at six that morning. But no rush today, he reminded himself, there was no appointment in the morning. He would go to his clinic later – maybe after a leisurely breakfast. Aditya snuggled close to Prachi and dozed off only to wake up a short while later with his cell phone ringing incessantly. He rubbed his eyes and peered at the phone. It was Jayant. Something rather unusual was up. Why is he calling early in the morning? He wondered.

'Hi, Jayant. Is everything okay?'

'Aditya, can you please come to Ramanagara right away?' Jayant sounded afraid and anxious.

'Now? But why? What happened?'

'It's my father-in-law.'

'What about him?'

'Yesterday, Smita and I picked up her parents from the railway station and came home. My father-in-law was fine at the time. However, after he woke up in the morning, he has been muttering nonsense non-stop. I thought it was a nightmare. But when it didn't subside, I called my neighbour; he is a retired general practitioner. He took one look and suggested that I contact a psychiatrist as soon as possible.'

Aditya glanced at the clock.

'It will take time to reach Ramanagara. Why don't you take him to an emergency room right away?'

'The doctor who saw him didn't say anything about immediate action. I think it's a panic attack or something like that and it will probably pass, but I will feel better if you see him rather than anybody else.' There was no trace of the uncivilised and loud-mouthed Jayant.

'Okay, I'll come, but tell me more,' Aditya said, as he walked to the bathroom with the phone to his ear.

'Smita's father is sixty-four. He exercises regularly and goes for yoga classes every other day. He has no other ailments apart from higher cholesterol for which he takes medicines. But there's a lot of pressure at work. After his retirement from a government college in Kolkata, he started teaching thrice a week in a private institution there. Maybe even those three days of work are too much–'

'Tell me more about today's incident,' Aditya interrupted.

'Well, we had dinner together last night and then he went to bed. Smita's parents usually wake up very early. At around five in the morning, her mother made tea and was surprised to find that he was still in bed. She tried to wake him up, but he did not open his eyes. He was breathing heavily and mumbling something incomprehensible. She got concerned and woke us up. When I called out to my father-in-law and patted his shoulder, he opened his eyes and sat up as if a livewire had touched him. Just as quickly, he burst out crying as if the world was about to end. I kept asking him what had happened…' Jayant paused to catch his breath.

'What did he say?'

'He shoved me aside and kept saying, "Go away. Don't touch me. Don't you dare come near me. Please go away." When I asked him if he was unwell, he said that there was no concept of being unwell in the state that he was in.'

'What state?'

'Apparently that of an unhappy soul. I didn't understand a word. He was weird. He kept repeating that he was an unhappy soul and that unhappy souls can harm living beings.'

'But does he seem otherwise okay except for the strange stuff he is telling?'

'Yes, he is. I asked him why he was an unhappy soul. He said that he didn't know why. He thought that he would go to heaven after his life ended, but instead, he was forced to hover around here. He started wailing after that. All this stuff about death and souls scared me. That's when I requested my neighbour to come over.'

'Let me get ready and come. You stay in the room with your father-in-law, but don't touch him or talk to him. Tell Smita and her mother to wait outside.'

Twenty minutes later, Aditya was on his way. The roads were empty and he was thankful for that. He drove quickly and reached Jayant's apartment in Ramanagara before the nine o'clock traffic hit the roads. When he walked in, he found Smita's father on the bed, sitting upright with his eyes closed.

Aditya sat down next to him.

'Hello, Uncle.'

Smita's father opened his eyes.

'Oh, it's you, Aditya. I'm so glad that you are here. Something dreadful has happened.'

'What happened, Uncle?'

'Can't you see? My soul is here, but I am no longer there. My body is gone. I'm only sixty-four. Is that any age to die?' His eyes became teary. He paused for a moment. 'When we reached here yesterday, everything was so nice. I wanted to relax and play with Litu, but my wife insisted on going to the market to buy chicken and some fruits. I didn't want to go. But she forced me to. On our way back from the market, we met with an accident and I died on the spot. I am sure my wife also died. Now, my daughter and my son-in-law are in complete denial.'

Aditya looked at Jayant.

Jayant whispered, 'It's true that they went to the market in a taxi. It's also correct that the driver was rash, but nothing untoward happened. They came back around seven. We had an early dinner, watched TV and an hour later all of us went to bed.'

'Okay.' Aditya nodded and turned his attention back to Smita's father.

'Uncle, I saw Aunty when I came into the apartment. She is very much here with us.'

'She has hoodwinked you. Believe me, she's dead and gone. Just like me. Smita and Jayant could not bear to part with us and have kept our bodies in the house. Our bodies are rotting here. I don't know about your aunty, but my soul is so unhappy that now I can't leave this world. Please counsel this young couple. It's not good to have a ghost hanging around. Nor should you keep rotting bodies in the house.'

He started sobbing.

Aditya let him be.

After a few minutes, the crying stopped and he screamed:

'Call somebody to do *Shanti Path* for me. Can't you organise this for me?'

Hearing his scream, Smita and her mother entered the room and stood near the door.

'It'll help me to let go, Aditya. I know you're a doctor. You do not believe in things like souls and ghosts. I used to be like you too. But now I know there is an alternate world – it exists.'

'Why are you talking about ghosts, Baba?' Smita could not take it anymore. She started sobbing.

'I am simply telling the truth.' He glared at her. 'Go away. Keep your husband and son away from your mother and me.'

Smita's mother interjected:

'Look, I'm right here in front of you. I am not a ghost. My body is not rotting.'

Her husband got agitated and flailed his arms.

'Who are you trying to fool? Go away. Smita is your only child. At least, don't harm her or her family.'

Aditya gestured everyone to step out of the room. The man needed to calm down. Once they were alone, he checked his pupils and then searched for a vein in his arm to give a dose of sedative. Aditya made him to lie down, comforting him while he worked, 'Everything will be all right, Uncle.'

'You think so?'

'Yes, I do.'

'How do you know that? Do you have some extraordinary power?'

'Maybe.'

'Tell me, when will things get a-l-r-i-g-h-t…' The words were slowed down.

'Are you feeling sleepy, Uncle?'

'Yes.'

'Why don't you nap for a while? I'm right here. We'll talk when you wake up.'

'Okay.' Smita's father closed his eyes and was fast asleep in a matter of minutes.

Aditya stepped out of the room. A visibly distraught Smita and her anxious mother were waiting. Her overactive seven-year-old son Litu also knew that something was not quite right and he was sitting silently at the dining table clutching a toy truck.

Aditya sat down on a chair next to him and Smita got him a glass of water from the kitchen.

'What happened to Baba?' she was shaken.

'He has a form of delusion. Medically, it is called nihilistic delusion. Cotard's Syndrome.'

'What's that?'

'There used to be a neurologist Jules Cotard, who described the condition as the "Delirium of Negation". It means a persistent denial of the existence of something. Patients strongly believe that they are dead, or putrefying, or that they don't exist. It becomes extremely difficult to make them believe otherwise.'

'Is it a kind of mental illness?'

'It is a neuro-psychiatric disorder.'

'Is it serious?'

'It can be. In a mild case, the patient has despair and self-loathing, but in a severe case, it can lead to chronic psychiatric depression.'

Smita's mother paled.

'But no one in our entire family has such a thing,' she remarked.

Jayant nodded in agreement.

'How many times have you heard mental problems being discussed? Most people are either in denial or secretive.'

'But why does it happen?' asked Smita.

'The causes are still unknown. And though it seems to happen unexpectedly, the ailment is really not sudden.'

Smita thought for a minute.

'Baba works in his garden regularly. Ma tells him repeatedly not to work in the unbearable Kolkata heat, but he never listens to her. Maybe the sun got to him.'

Aditya had learnt to have patience with over-simplification.

'No, Smita, I don't think that was the cause. Working in the garden could have only led to a heat stroke; it can't cause a delusional disorder.'

'Well, what do we do now?'

'He needs to be treated.' Aditya turned to Smita's mother, 'Aunty, how long can you stay here?'

'Not long. Smita's father has taken ten days off from work to come here for Litu's birthday. I'm sure that he can extend it by a few days and Jayant can re-book the train tickets, but we can't stay here for longer than that.'

'Aunty, you must not delay the treatment.'

'Can you take care of it, then? Will ten or twelve days be enough? We can catch a flight instead of taking the train,' Smita's mother replied.

'Aunty, I'll start the treatment right away, but Uncle will not recover completely in ten days. You will need to find a psychiatrist in Kolkata who can monitor him.'

'Are you sure that he really needs a psychiatrist?' she asked. She was afraid of the social implication.

'Yes, Aunty.'

'But we don't know any psychiatrist in Kolkata,' she said feebly.

'Do you have a family doctor?'

'Not really. We only go to a lady doctor near our house if we need something.'

'Then ask her to recommend someone.'

'Okay, I'll try, but will your Uncle become absolutely fine with the treatment?'

'It will take time.' Aditya was brief. It would dissuade her if he told her that it wasn't easy to treat such a disorder. If someone firmly believed in the existence of something that was not there, or vice versa, it was a difficult task. There has been a lot of serious research on the subject, but a comprehensive treatment isn't quite there.

When Aditya was doing his post-graduation, he had treated some cases of delusions and a few that were nihilistic. He recalled Sunil – the eldest child of a lower-middle-class family who believed that he was not an Indian; he thought that he was a Russian. Sunil's father had explained that his son had always loved Russian history. One day, Sunil started believing that he was Tsar Nicolai, or rather his ghost, and that he had not been executed but that he had died of AIDS.

Then there was a young twenty-eight-year-old girl, whose colleague had brought her in without a prior appointment. Aditya still remembered the girl's terrified eyes. She had told him:

'There is a lot of office politics where I work. Everybody is jealous of me because I am a good employee. Now, my co-workers are trying to scare me so that I leave voluntarily.'

'But what did they do?'

She sighed.

'There used to be a mongrel outside our office. One day, he was crossing the road and got run over by a truck. I heard that the office people buried the body, but it was a lie. When I came to office the next day, I found the dead dog hanging from a fan in the centre of the room. I tried not to look and walked to my desk only to find blood all over it. I screamed in terror and people around me just laughed. They thought that it was very funny. After that incident, I'd find some dead carcass or the other near my desk every day.' The girl started crying loudly.

The whole thing was a delusion. It had taken some time to calm the girl. While she was leaving, Aditya told her to come again in a few days, but she never did.

Later, her colleague had phoned Aditya and told him that she had resigned from her job and moved away with her parents to a village. Aditya never found out what happened to her. He only hoped that she got treatment, because she was dangerously unwell.

'Is this... this nihilistic delusion that you are talking about... is it dangerous?' Jayant asked Aditya a question for the first time since he had walked in.

'It could be. It takes its toll on both the patient and the family. There is a famous case of a young man who had a bike accident and then thought he was dead. When his mother took him from Edinburgh to some place in Africa, which was hot and humid, he was convinced that he had reached hell. What's confusing is that this syndrome appears suddenly in people who have had no previous psychiatric history.'

'What is our best option for treatment?' Smita's mother was anxious.

'We have to ensure that this does not get out of control. That's why I recommend that a psychiatrist should monitor Uncle on a regular basis. Aunty, you must take charge.'

Smita's mother looked away.

'It's going to be really difficult to find someone discreet,' she mumbled.

The issue of discretion again! Somehow, it always mattered more than a patient's treatment!

'I'll check and let you know,' Aditya said. 'If you like, I can stay in contact with the psychiatrist in Kolkata.'

Smita and her mother relaxed a little at his suggestion.

'What will happen after he wakes up?' Jayant wondered.

'Let's wait and see.'

'Can you please stay till then?' Smita implored.

'I will. I've given Uncle a small dose of sedative that will wear off soon,' Aditya said as he took out his cell phone. He needed to inform Prachi.

***

Smita's father woke up after a couple of hours.

'Smita, give me some tea. I've slept for so long. Why didn't you wake me up earlier?'

It was then he saw Aditya in the room.

'Ah, when did you come?'

'Just a while ago, Uncle. How are you?'

'I'm fine.' He paused. 'Please excuse me. I'll brush my teeth first. My mouth feels funny.'

Though he sounded normal, Aditya knew that the relief was only temporary.

Smita's mother brightened when she saw her husband walk to the bathroom.

'See? He's fine now. It must have been because of a lack of rest, or his nightmare last night. Aditya, do we still need to see a psychiatrist?' she asked.

Aditya was firm.

'Aunty, you shouldn't ignore this. It definitely needs more investigation.'

'Are you sure?'

'Absolutely.' He turned to Jayant. 'Can you bring him to my clinic in the evening, maybe around six? I'd like to get his blood work done in a lab nearby.'

Smita's mother became annoyed.

'If it's a matter of getting the blood work done, we can do that around here in Ramanagara. Why does he need to go to a psychiatrist's clinic? He's not mad. He just needs to rest.'

Even the thick-skinned Jayant was mortified at her outburst, but Aditya did not take offence. He was quite used to people reacting in anger; it was just another form of denial. He replied patiently.

'Aunty, psychiatry is not only about the mentally ill. Sometimes a normal, average mind needs attention, just like any other part of the body.'

'Oh, I see,' she said. It was clear that she did not see.

Jayant intervened.

'Ma, I think it's better to get at least one expert opinion. It'll do no harm and it will make us feel better, too.'

'Fine,' she said, somewhat resigned, and walked into the kitchen.

Aditya had an intuition that Smita's father would not come to see him in the evening. He was right. Jayant was very uncomfortable when he conveyed his wife and mother-in-law's decision about not coming to the clinic.

Aditya tried to put him at ease.

'That's alright, Jayant. Since they are leaving for Kolkata soon, they can visit a doctor there. Why don't I give you a Kolkata-based psychiatrist's name and number? I met her in one of our conferences. She has written a paper on delusion.'

'Let me find a pen.'

Aditya gave the psychiatrist's details on the phone. He was sure that Jayant would pass on the information to his in-laws, but he also knew from past experience that Smita's mother would resist taking her husband there. He knew many people who behaved like her; they didn't perceive the enormity of the problem and most times, they refused to even acknowledge the existence of one. That evening, Aditya was pensive as he walked back home after finishing all his work at the clinic. Once home, he lightened up at the sight of Prachi in the kitchen. She made him tea and they talked about how the day had gone.

Later that evening, Prachi got busy with a few phone calls and Aditya went to his study to open Deepa's second journal.

11

Deepa met Ethan when she started working at a retail store; he was her manager. Ethan was recovering from an ugly divorce and welcomed the conversations with Deepa during breaks, sometimes over a cup of coffee or a meal. She was grateful to have finally found a friend who listened to her without being judgemental. Initially, she found it difficult to talk about Naren, but gradually, she was able to confide in Ethan, in bits and pieces, until he became completely aware of the messy situation that she was in. He gave her strength to go home and tackle her problems. They were just two people trying to alleviate their loneliness. At best, the relationship was platonic.

Then came the day when Naren died. The tragic incident involved a police investigation, court appearances and transfer of property issues, among many other complications. Life overwhelmed Deepa; the solitary life meant she had no one to turn to. That was when Ethan offered her a helping hand. He stood by her side for days at a stretch so that she could retain her sanity and deal with the problems and uncertainties. What really touched Deepa was that Ethan and Raj got along really well. Raj started looking forward to Ethan's visits.

Gradually she started seeing Ethan more often, until one day when he stayed over and spent the weekend in her house. For the first time in her life, Deepa felt the exhilaration of giving herself completely. With her Indian upbringing, she had assumed that romance was only for the young, and yearning and lust in a woman who was on the wrong side of forty was rare and ridiculous. It was wonderful to be wrong. That weekend, Deepa fell in love with Ethan. Finally, after years of turmoil, her life was going to be content and joyful.

Deepa, however, was in no hurry to take the relationship to the next level. She was weary and scared of burning her fingers a second time. Ethan was also cautious; his earlier divorce had left quite a bitter taste in his mouth. Months went by. With time, their relationship grew stronger. Then one day, when they had gone to the Lake District on a long weekend, Ethan proposed to her and Deepa happily accepted. She was over the moon.

***

The wedding was to take place soon, since there was no need for either of them to wait, but destiny's hand changed their plans. Ethan had a skiing accident that left him in a critical condition for weeks. Though it was not life threatening, he was confined to the bed. The doctors said that his recovery could take almost a year. There was no question of a wedding and the date was pushed back indefinitely. Between Deepa's work and daily visits to Ethan, she failed to notice the gradual change in her son, and the day she did, it struck her like a thunderbolt. She was devastated.

***

Deepa got complaints from the new school: Raj was picking fights with other students and refusing to obey the principal and his teachers.

She confronted Raj, 'Why are you behaving like this?'

'They insist, Mama,' he shot back.

'Who?' Deepa was irritated, convinced that her son was in bad company.

'I can't see them, but they are always around me, watching me and talking very loudly about me. I can hear their voices clearly.'

An alarm bell went off in Deepa's head and she was reminded of the psychiatrist's question during Naren's first visit to the hospital after the shopping aisle incident. He had asked her, 'Does Naren ever talk about hearing voices?'

Deepa had said truthfully at that time that her husband did not, but he always complained that people were watching him and plotting to make his life miserable. Now the same words from Raj! Deepa gazed at her son and felt a chill, but she tried to rationalise, to find an explanation. Maybe the voices were the result of an overactive imagination or maybe he was just acting out. The teenager needed to be guided through what might be a confusing phase. So she worked on him; sometimes cajoling, sometimes being tough, but nothing helped. Eventually, Raj was asked to leave the school at the end of the year.

Unfortunately, Deepa could not share Raj's issues with a recuperating Ethan, who himself was on painkillers and was sometimes wallowing in self-pity. He expected Deepa's time and attention, unaware of what she was going through.

***

She poured her heart out in the journal. This was her way of coping with her problems. Aditya turned the page. Raj's exit from school and her inability to communicate with Ethan was her last entry. Thereafter the pages were blank. Her emotions had probably pushed her to the brink and she returned to Bangalore, desperately trying to find a solution.

Aditya closed the journal.

There were missing portions in the chronicle and he understood why. Sometimes, events and emotions are so disturbing that it is easier to keep them locked in the mind somewhere and throw the keys away. Do they ever fade away or do they simply merge with the subconscious only to raise their heads at a later day? Aditya knew that she needed a therapist, but unfortunately, people like her didn't think so.

***

Prachi's call for dinner woke up Aditya from his reverie. As he walked over to the dining room, he wondered about Ethan. He had been a pillar of strength and a ray of light for Deepa and Raj. What happened to him?

Aditya could only guess. He had seen so much heartache, unimaginable misery and the urge to escape. The trauma of mental disorder was devastating for the person enduring it, but it was worse for the caregiver, who found it difficult to fathom the pain and watch a loved one suffer. Unable to cope with the demands that come with handling such patients, he had come across cases of children being abandoned, wives deserted by tired husbands and distressed wives opting for separation.

Ethan probably ended the relationship with Deepa.

Aditya's heart went out to her. He tried to imagine her anguish. The days and nights must have been hell. It was clear from her journal that she was in denial, and that was why she had not taken her son to a psychiatrist. Instead, she ran away from a scary world and brought him here.

Aditya continued to be in a pensive mood at dinner. He didn't quite know what he was eating. Prachi was used to her husband's occasional inattentiveness when he was thinking deeply about a case and she rarely got upset. She watched him as he finished his dinner absent-mindedly, walked out to their courtyard and just sat down staring into nothingness.

As usual, Prachi joined him a few minutes later with two cups of hot chocolate. It was a daily routine, except when they had guests staying over. After their marriage, Prachi had moved Aditya away from his two terrible pre-bedtime habits – cigarettes and black coffee. Both had been replaced with hot chocolate. Aditya sipped his drink without saying a word. Prachi tried to initiate a conversation, but it was so one-sided that she gave up and looked at the plants around her.

Unlike other houses on the street, their home did not have a garden, but its absence was somewhat made up by a large courtyard. The previous owners had used the space as their utility area. However, Prachi and Aditya decided to overhaul it after moving in. The drab courtyard had now become the most cheerful place in their home, filled with potted crotons and seasonal flowers. Lush creepers with orange flowers covered a trellis leading up to the roof. They had a gardener who came everyday to water the potted plants, but it was really Prachi's love that made a huge difference.

Prachi took Aditya's hand in hers and asked again, 'You've been distracted for almost a week now. What's going on? Is it Prakash, or are you worried about a patient?'

Aditya knew if he didn't say anything she wouldn't take offence. She respected his profession and the need for confidentiality that came with it. But right now, he felt a need to share his concerns; to use her as a sounding board. He wondered if it would be awkward to mention Deepa, even though he had told Prachi about her before they got married. It really made no sense for him to feel uncomfortable about discussing Deepa at this stage of his life; she simply happened to be his patient's mother and his friend's cousin.

'Prakash was not looking for a psychiatrist for himself; it was for Deepa's son,' he said.

'Deepa?' Prachi was surprised. 'Didn't she go away to London?'

'She did. But she is in Bangalore these days and her son probably has schizophrenia. I think that he's inherited it from his father.'

Prachi was shocked.

'Deepa was married to someone with schizophrenia?'

'Well, nobody knew when she got married. Her husband was diagnosed later and he struggled with the disorder. Eventually, he committed suicide. Now, her son is also exhibiting similar behaviour.'

Aditya saw the pain in his wife's eyes.

'I wish Deepa didn't have a child,' he blurted out.

Prachi was taken aback.

'How can you say something like that? Look at us!'

'I don't know what is worse. Not having a child, or seeing your child suffer. Deepa's life is such a mess.'

'Aditya, whatever the situation may be, I don't expect someone like you to make such a comment. I treat many children every day and they come to me with myriads of illnesses – some are inherited and some are not. Do you really think that not having a child is an actual option for most people? What about the pain of childlessness?'

'Sorry, Prachi, I've been reading Deepa's journal and it has really affected me.'

'I have read blogs of children whose parents have schizophrenia and it is heart-wrenching. Yes, there are some who are upset with their parents for bringing them into this life and dragging them into the messy world of schizophrenia, but then there are others who are willing to take charge of their life. They know that it can be managed if they follow medical advice. Still, how does that give anyone the right to try and control nature and tell people to stop having babies?'

'You are right,' Aditya conceded. 'I see cases where the parents and grandparents are absolutely normal and the child has a mental disorder. Sometimes, there is a long-forgotten gene that runs in the family and sometimes, there's no apparent reason at all.'

'Why is it taking so much research and time to find an effective drug for schizophrenia?' Prachi sounded frustrated.

'It may not happen during our lifetime, but some day, someone will solve the puzzle. For now, we have made at least some progress that allows us to keep the problem in check.'

Prachi nodded and looked at Aditya.

'You miss research, don't you?' she asked.

'Sometimes; but most of the time, I think of my practice as a non-trivial service. Someone has to do it. If I am successful in helping people lead a normal life, it is a great thing.'

'Why can't one do research alongside treating patients? I'm not talking about a big, government institution. I'm talking about a private setup with like-minded people, where the profits could be used to fund research. Can't you start something like that?'

Aditya looked at his wife. That thought had come to him many times, but he was hesitant. A private clinic was different from running a research organisation. He was not sure if he had it in him.

'It's not easy to build something like that. Apart from dedication, you need financial acumen. You need a lot of management, a lot of support,' he heard himself say.

'You have all those, Aditya.'

He was flattered. He put his arms around his wife and asked, 'If I start something like that, will you join me?'

It was Prachi's turn to be hesitant.

'I am not sure. I have never seen myself as an entrepreneur. You know what I mean?'

'If we have our own organisation, we can complement each other.'

'You really think so?'

'Yes, of course. And you have so much compassion and sensitivity.'

Prachi was a little embarrassed by such praise.

'You have those qualities as well.'

'Oh, tell me more about my qualities,' now Aditya teased her.

There was mischief in her eyes.

'Aha! Are we fishing for compliments here?'

'Maybe. No, seriously, what else do you see in me?'

'Shut up! I don't see anything good in you. You are bad, bad, bad.' Prachi yawned and tugged at his hand. 'Let's go to bed. I'm feeling sleepy.'

12

Aditya entered the clinic and wondered if Deepa and Raj would come to his clinic today, or would she cancel the appointment like Jayant's in-laws had? Deepa had seen the horrors of mental illness from up close, and hopefully, that would prevent her from being in denial, especially since the patient was her son.

Aditya's first patient that morning was Tanushree. Her progress in all these months had been marvellous. He was correct in his initial diagnosis and she had been immediately started on a lithium routine. But what she also needed was regular intense therapy. Thankfully, Tanushree was a very organised and methodical person and she had been doing her bit very sincerely. As Aditya and Tanushree sat down for a review that morning, he felt very pleased with her progress and they signed up on the follow up schedule.

His phone rang soon after Tanushree left. It was Deepa.

'Hi, are you back in Bangalore?' he answered the call.

'Yes, we came back last night.' She paused. 'Did you read my journals?'

'Yes.'

'So now you know everything about Naren and how much I suffered,' she said softly.

'I do. But Deepa, has it ever crossed your mind that the man who caused you so much suffering also suffered much himself?'

There was silence at the other end of the line. Deepa mulled over the statement.

'I think you're right. I shouldn't forget that there were times before his illness progressed, when he was normal. Actually more than that – he was also caring and considerate,' she said haltingly.

'Tell me, didn't the doctors tell you about the genetic factors associated with this disorder? If a parent has schizophrenia, the child has a more than average likelihood of inheriting some form of mental disorder.'

'Naren's psychiatrist had warned me and told me to be vigilant with Raj. I tried. I really did, but I've probably failed in my duty towards him.'

'Deepa, please don't beat yourself up. Sometimes, even trained professionals fail in these matters.'

'But why did this happen, Aditya? I have never harmed anyone. Why is God so unkind? I wish I had known about these things before having Raj. I would never have brought a child into this mess.'

Aditya was taken aback – he had said the very same words to Prachi the night before.

'Please don't say that, Deepa. You've got to move on. I hope that you are bringing Raj for our appointment today.'

'I don't know. I'm not sure. What will I do if he throws a tantrum and creates a scene in your clinic?'

'Don't worry about that. I'll handle it,' Aditya offered.

Suddenly, Deepa sounded bitter.

'What's the use of treating him? I did everything I could for Naren. Many doctors gave us assurances, but he committed suicide in the end. I've read a few articles on the Internet. They say that when this happens to young children, the parents feel like they have lost their child to the disease.'

The curse of too much information.

'If you have read this,' Aditya responded, 'then you must have also read that there is a course of action available for the illness. People who take the prescribed anti-psychotic drugs and attend their therapy sessions regularly can function normally in society and even pursue a career.'

Deepa was not ready to give in.

'Yes, I read that too. But a website said that only one-third of the diagnosed patients are able to live normally after their treatment. Another one-third may go into relapse, and the remaining one-third is unable to function at all. What if Raj falls in the last category?'

'And what if he falls in the first? How would you know which category he belongs to if you don't get him treated at all?'

She didn't reply.

'We have to try, Deepa. We cannot give up. Or do you prefer that Raj suffers all by himself without help?'

That question struck a chord. She took a deep breath and felt calmer.

'I will treat Raj and he should be able to live his life on his own. Have faith in me,' Aditya assured her.

There was no response from Deepa.

'Had Raj been a heart patient or a diabetic, would you have been averse to treatment? Would you not have gone for the best medical advice?'

'How can you compare those illnesses to a mental disorder? People don't scorn you when you are diagnosed with diabetes or a heart ailment.'

As a psychiatrist, Aditya was only too aware of the problem.

'I agree that our society does not accept mental illnesses as a disability or a disease, but that does not mean that you or I should refuse to seek medical attention. The brain is also a part of our body.'

'Raj would have to be on medication all his life,' she said in despair.

'He would have to do that if he had diabetes. Trust me, this is the only way to keep the disorder in check.'

'Then prescribe the medicines and I'll make sure that Raj takes them.'

'It does not work that way, Deepa.' Aditya proceeded to explain how the disorder is treatable, but that every patient is different. A psychiatrist will not write a prescription without getting to know the person first. Different combinations of medications need to be tried out.

'So you think Raj will be alright if he takes medicines? Would he become perfect?'

Aditya was truthful:

'I am yet to understand the definition of a perfect person or life. All I can say for sure is that life will be more manageable for Raj and you if he gets treated.' He paused for a few seconds, 'So, will I see you today?'

'Okay, we will be there at five.'

'Can you make it five-thirty? I have an appointment at 4:30 p.m. for a half-hour, but it may spill over.'

***

The 4:30 p.m. appointment was for Shabnam. But well before her time, it started raining around noon. What began as a light drizzle changed into an unseasonal lashing that brought the city to a standstill. Aditya wondered if Shabnam would show up with her husband Ali for the appointment at four-thirty.

She did. Despite the heavy rain, she did come on time with her husband. Years of excesses had stripped Ali of whatever nature had once bestowed upon him in terms of good looks and health. He looked sick and somewhat unpleasant. It was going to be a tough session, but Aditya was ready.

As they settled down in Aditya's chamber, Ali glared at him and snapped, 'Okay, tell me.'

'Why don't you tell me?' Aditya looked the man in his eyes.

'I don't have the time. Whatever you have to say, say it quickly.'

'I am here only to listen. Tell me, what's bothering you?' Aditya waited for the outburst.

It happened right away. Ali kicked the chair near him and screamed:

'Bloody hell, you pretend to be a doctor, but you want to break my family apart? Why are you teaching my wife to revolt against me? She has the audacity to threaten me and say that she will complain to the police if I don't come here and meet you.'

Aditya remained calm.

The man growled and cursed and fumed. After he was spent, he asked in a hoarse voice, 'Why don't *you* tell me if there is anything wrong?'

'My job is to listen to you first,' Aditya repeated. 'Tell me, what's bothering you?'

'Who said that anything was bothering me? I am fit as a fiddle. The only thing that I can think of is my bad luck to be burdened with such a wife, who refuses to do her duty. Obviously, I have to find other means of satisfying myself.'

'Are you talking about visiting prostitutes?'

'Do I really have an option? Whores don't have any pretensions. Pay money and enjoy yourself any which way you want.' He laughed in an evil way.

'So you don't bother anyone else?'

'Why should I? I go to whores and spend my money. I don't take charity from anyone.' He looked at his wife pointedly. 'Has she been complaining to you?'

'No. But there are enough women waiting in line to complain against you including your neighbours.'

Ali lost his nerve. He stared at Aditya in shock.

'If you think that you will face only the police, you are mistaken. You may lose your job. Your entire family, everyone, will be taken to court. The media will know. Soon, you will be all over the newspapers and become a subject of public interest.'

All the bluster vanished. The man slumped.

'Would you please wait outside?' Aditya asked Shabnam.

The moment his wife walked out of the room, Ali started talking. His problem began when he was a teenager. It was natural for him to be curious about a woman's body at that age, but over time, he became obsessed with it.

When he was young, his family lived in a house rented out to six different families that shared the three common bathrooms on the property. Ali became a Peeping Tom and watched the women in the bathrooms. The young boy was caught a few times and got into trouble with the families.

Amidst all that, Ali somehow managed to complete his graduation and found a government job.

That was when Shabnam happened.

Shabnam's brother was his friend and he used that pretext to visit their house regularly. He got bolder with time and brought along pornographic magazines, when he knew that the fifteen-year-old would be alone at home. One day, Shabnam lost restraint and gave in to Ali. Unfortunately, she became pregnant and could not hide the truth from her family, who in turn, informed Ali's parents. Both the families forced him to get married to the pregnant Shabnam and take responsibility for the unborn child.

He married her, but that did not change anything. Instead, he held her responsible for tying him down. Shabnam endured physical violence and unnatural sexual demands for years. After she became the mother of two sons, Ali lost interest in her and began preying on other young women.

When he was caught exposing himself to their neighbour's teenage daughter, he was beaten to a pulp. So he decided that it was better to visit prostitutes.

'Do you realise that such thoughts and actions are abnormal?' asked Aditya.

There was no response.

'You have an illness and I can help. But I can't do it without your cooperation. First, you have to go for therapy. I have to put you on medication later, after a few tests.'

'I'm not going anywhere. I don't have money.'

'Don't worry about money. I am treating you for free. If at all, it's my time that's getting wasted.'

Ali was incensed.

'Are you telling me that I'm here on charity? I don't need your bloody charity.'

Aditya buzzed Aruna and asked her to send Shabnam in.

When Shabnam walked in, he told her, 'Your husband needs to go for therapy, but before that, a few tests need to be done. I'll speak to Dr Das. He was the one who sent you here. Bring your husband back in two weeks.'

Before Shabnam could respond, Ali shouted:

'I am not going to come back. There's nothing wrong with me.' He gave his wife a threatening glare, 'By the way, I will take care of you at home.'

Aditya pointed a finger at him and spoke in a deliberately cold tone.

'If you do anything to her – anything at all, I will be the first person to call the police and give testimony in court.'

Ali gave him a sour look and marched out of the door with a distraught Shabnam trailing after him.

Aditya took a few deep breaths to calm his mind. He would have preferred a simple explanation to Ali's appalling behaviour. He would have understood had the underlying cause been childhood trauma or victimisation from a sexual predator. Then the solution would have been simple therapy. Regrettably, Aditya knew that it was not going to be that way. He suspected that there was a possibility of acute chemical imbalance, which would need months of treatment and close monitoring.

He wasn't sure if the man was ready for that.

13

Aditya buzzed Aruna and she ushered Deepa and Raj inside.

'I'm sorry about the wait,' apologised Aditya.

'That's not a problem at all. I always seem to come to your clinic at the wrong time.' She had obviously seen Ali walk out in a huff.

Aditya shrugged.

'It's not usual, but these things happen sometimes. It's a professional hazard, I guess.'

He gazed at Raj, who was dressed casually in a grey t-shirt and stonewashed jeans and appeared to be in perfect health. Aditya smiled at him.

'Hello, Raj.'

'Hi, Uncle, I didn't know that you were a doctor. I somehow thought that Prakash Uncle and you were in high school together.'

'No, we met in medical college.'

'Yes, Mama said so. You wanted to talk to me?' Raj seemed coherent and aware.

'Yes, why don't we?'

Raj leaned forward and said conspiratorially, 'You want to discuss Bobby, right?'

Aditya nodded.

'Oh good! That boy really needs help. He's making life miserable for everyone and I'm the one who always gets into trouble. Can you please do something for him and make him better?'

'I hope so.' Aditya turned to Deepa, 'Would you mind waiting outside? I'd like to talk to Raj alone.'

Deepa did not like the idea, but she went out quietly.

'So, tell me. What's going on?' Aditya asked.

Immediately, Raj started speaking. He spoke non-stop, barely pausing to catch his breath.

'When I was twelve, I found a boy hiding under a table in our garden shed in London. He told me that his name was Bobby and that he was the same age as me. When I asked him, he said he had run away from his home in Dover because his mom and stepdad didn't treat him well. He begged me not to tell my mother in case she turned him over to the police. At first, I felt sorry for him and didn't tell my mother. He lived in the shed for a few days. Then he started creating trouble.'

'What kind of trouble?'

'He damaged the plants and spoilt our garden completely. Then he broke the windowpanes for no reason. Mama was very upset. She thought that I was doing all that. I warned Bobby, but he wouldn't listen to me. In fact, he became worse. I was shocked when he started torturing our neighbours' pets.'

'Why didn't you stop him?' questioned Aditya.

'I couldn't. People warned me against telling him anything,' said Raj nonchalantly.

'Which people?'

'I don't know them. Actually, I can't even see them. I just hear their voices all the time.' He swallowed. 'Can I have some water, please?'

'Sure.' Aditya poured water into a glass and noticed that the narrative scared Raj.

'What did you do after that?' he nudged the boy further.

'One day Mama got to know about Bobby. When she asked me, I told her everything. She was stunned. I felt bad, but was helpless. Soon Bobby started following me to school and created trouble there: he slapped the boys and shoved the girls. And do you know what happened? The teachers thought that I was the culprit. I tried to explain, but nobody listened. And then, the principal asked me to leave the school.'

Raj paused for a while and smiled.

'It wasn't a bad idea at all. The school was boring and the students were dumb. Mama transferred me to another school. But it was worse than the last one. Thank goodness, I was asked to leave the new school as well. I wanted to study at home, but Mama didn't agree. Then she told me that we should move to India. In a different country with new people, maybe Bobby would behave himself and I agreed with her.'

'So you were happy to come to India?' Aditya was surprised.

'Yes.'

'And is Bobby better here?'

'No, nothing has changed. He continues to break things here as well and makes a mess in our house. He doesn't like going out to play with other kids. He does not understand their accent. I really don't know how to handle him. Whenever I try to tell him anything, the voices...'

'Are you still hearing the voices?'

Raj's face became pale.

'Please don't tell Mama. Will you help me, please?' he pleaded.

Schizophrenia. There was no doubt at all.

'I'll try my best, Raj.' Aditya was gentle.

'Thank you.'

'Raj, please wait outside and send your mother in.'

Seconds later, Deepa came in looking anxious, as if she was waiting to hear the verdict.

'It's schizophrenia,' Aditya did not want to sugar-coat the diagnosis.

'Are you… are you sure?'

'Yes. I need to run a few tests before deciding the line of treatment. Aruna will tell you where you can get them done. After I get the report, I'll prescribe the medicines and the dosage, but we will need to monitor Raj over time. I may have to increase or decrease the dosage, or change the combination. Also, it is equally important to see a psychologist. Therapy is crucial for…'

'A shrink? Are you saying that Raj has to visit a shrink? Come on, Aditya. Why can't he talk to you?'

'I can only take care of Raj's physical problems, but a therapist will be able to help him deal with his deep and disturbing thoughts. There's no formula that fits all. Each case is different and a good therapist works all his cases differently. It's a lot of work.'

Deepa took a few minutes to respond.

'Aditya, please tell me the truth. If Raj follows your advice, will he be cured?'

'Raj's illness can definitely be managed. You have to keep faith. You must do your best and ensure that both the medicines and therapy are regular. If you'd like, I can set up an appointment with a therapist whom I've known for years. Her name is Anjana Singh. She's very good at her job and I work with her often.'

Deepa nodded as she stood up to leave.

'I'll call you.'

***

She phoned three days later and agreed to try out Aditya's recommended course of treatment.

Immediately, Aditya spoke to Anjana who agreed to take on Raj's case and scheduled his first visit to her office on Saturday.

Aditya called Deepa back and updated her.

'Raj's appointment with Anjana is on Saturday. Why don't you take down her office phone number and address?'

'Okay, tell me,' she said disinterestedly.

Aditya ignored her apathy as he gave her Anjana's details. He was aware of the turmoil that she was going through and sympathised with it. He was about to hang up when a thought struck him.

'Deepa, how do you spend your time during the day?' he asked.

She was not expecting such a question and paused for a moment before replying.

'I don't really do anything in particular. Why do you ask?'

He hesitated, but decided to take the plunge.

'Since you may have some free time, why don't you consider volunteering for an organisation?'

'No, Aditya, I don't have the energy or the inclination to work right now.' Deepa sounded tired.

'It's not a full-time job. I have a friend, Jonathan Das; he runs a non-profit social organisation. He works with people from the lower middle class and educates them about mental problems. He encourages them to overcome stigma and obtain help through therapy. The organisation has its own counsellors and a therapist, but when things become unmanageable or they feel that someone needs to see a psychiatrist, they send the person to me. Even Anjana Singh volunteers there once a week.'

'But I am neither a psychiatrist nor a therapist and I am not qualified to be a social worker.'

'It doesn't matter. Jonathan, the founder, is an academician. He takes evening classes at a private college. He used to be an Assistant Professor of History at the University, but he gave it up in order to start the non-profit organisation and work there during the day. Do you know why?'

Deepa was silent.

'It's because he wants to help other people. He suffers from a mental disorder himself and openly talks about it with other people so that they will come forward. You won't realise it when you meet him, but he suffers from bipolar disorder and has to be on medication for rest of his life.'

'So?' She was not impressed, 'Maybe he's comfortable talking about his journey and problems, but I'm not ready to talk to people about Naren, and certainly not about Raj.'

'I'm not asking you to do that, Deepa. Nor would Jonathan. He will not probe into your personal life,' Aditya said confidently. 'The first step is to simply listen to people. Jonathan has a few helpers, but he could use somebody who's educated, sympathetic and aware of this field – someone like you. You don't have to tell him about Naren or Raj. Join him as a volunteer and I assure you that this will be therapeutic and meaningful for you too.'

She thought about it for a moment.

'It's probably a good idea to get out of the house and do something worthwhile. But what if I am unable to go regularly? You know that things can be unpredictable in my life.'

'I know and that's why I suggested Jonathan's organisation. The environment is informal and transparent. Since you will be doing voluntary service, your timings could also be flexible.'

'It may just work.' Deepa sounded positive.

'I think it will. Would you like me to talk to Jonathan?'

'Sure. Yes, please do. As I said, it may be a good idea for me to get out of the house for a while every day,' Deepa said, before saying goodbye and hanging up.

14

Jonathan's organisation, Manas, was located close to Bangalore's famous Bull Temple. It was a three-roomed outhouse in the large compound of what was now a rundown house his father had once built. Years of disuse had stripped the place of the charm that it once had; the iron gate was rusty and the fence in disrepair. Amidst all of this, stood a huge gulmohur tree laden with flowers, as if to reassure those walking in.

Deepa stood at the small signboard in front of the building, unsure of what to expect. She wondered if she had been too quick to agree when Jonathan had phoned her two nights ago.

She entered the building and looked around the room. It was supposed to be the reception area. A few chairs were scattered around and there were about a dozen people. They looked quite normal.

'Hello, may I help you?' a young girl in an ordinary blue *salwar-kameez* asked her pleasantly.

'Is Dr Jonathan Das there?'

The girl held out a register.

'Yes, but I need to write down your name. He meets people on a first-come, first-served basis.'

Deepa was confused.

'I'm sorry, but he was the one who asked me to come this morning at nine.'

'Aren't you here for counselling?'

'No, I want to volunteer.'

'Oh, I'm so sorry.' The young girl smiled apologetically. 'I will let Jonathan Sir know that you are here. May I know your name please?'

'Deepa.'

'Please take a seat. He's with someone right now, but it shouldn't take long.'

'That's no problem. I'll wait.'

She located an empty chair, sat down and picked up an old issue of a news magazine. She flipped through the pages, but found her eyes skimming over the people in the waiting room. Just as she had noticed the first time, none of them looked unwell, except for a middle-aged woman who seemed nervous and fidgety. Did she need help herself or was she worried about the man sitting next to her?

'Ma'am, Jonathan Sir will see you now,' said the pleasant young woman and led her to Jonathan's office.

As Deepa entered the room, Jonathan got up from his chair. He was a handsome man, dressed casually in a white linen shirt, sleeves rolled up, over a pair of khaki cotton trousers.

'Good morning. Welcome to Manas.'

'Thanks, Dr Das.'

'Jonathan. Please call me Jonathan.'

'Jonathan,' Deepa said as she sat down, 'I have no experience in your field and I really don't know how I could assist you.'

'Don't think that we only have highly qualified volunteers here. Most of them have joined us because they really want to help. Some of them have a lot of potential and we train them to be counsellors. The training is for four months, followed by a three-month apprenticeship. Since you come with Aditya's recommendation, I know that you will be a valued asset. I am hoping that you'd like to be a counsellor.'

'How can such a short course qualify me to become a therapist?'

'Not a therapist, Deepa, a counsellor.'

She looked baffled.

'Isn't it the same?'

'Ah, let me explain. There's a subtle difference between the two. Counsellors usually address a particular problem and give advice on how to deal with it. A therapist, on the other hand, tries to understand a person's thought process and the subconscious. Simply put, counselling requires lesser skill than psychotherapy. I was talking to you about the former.'

'Oh, I didn't know that.' Deepa wondered, 'Do you think that I can really do it? What if I can't make it to the class on a regular basis?'

'Then you'll just take a few extra days to train,' Jonathan said softly. 'Are you ready to see the office now? There's not much to see, but you will get a sense… Neelima!' he called.

The girl in the blue *salwar-kameez* walked in.

'Neelima, will you please show Deepa around, give her a cup of coffee and explain the paper work? I will join her in a moment.'

Deepa got up from her chair and followed Neelima out of the room. The veranda of the outhouse had been turned into a reception area. There were two private rooms for counsellors and a smaller room for the therapist. The enclosed space in the back of the house was a staff room consisting only of a square table and four plastic chairs. There was a large thermos flask on the table with paper cups next to it.

'Coffee?' Neelima asked as she walked up to the table.

'Half a cup please.' She sat down on a chair nearby. 'May I ask you a question?'

'Sure.' Neelima poured out coffee in two cups.

'The people in the waiting room – are they all here for counselling?'

'Yes.'

'But… but they look so normal.'

'I know. But looks can be so misleading. Sometimes the horror stories from people desperately seeking counsel will make anyone's stomach churn. I am sure Jonathan Sir will soon tell you all about that. Here we are trained to be strong at heart,' Neelima said as she opened a cupboard, took out some papers and put them in front of Deepa.

Deepa stared apprehensively at the pile of papers. This was her training material.

She looked at the young Neelima and asked, 'Have you completed this course?'

'No, I haven't studied much. I barely finished middle school.'

'Then how are you...' Deepa checked herself and said, 'never mind.' She shouldn't be asking any personal questions.

'Do you mean how I came to work in this office?' Neelima offered. 'I brought my younger brother for treatment here and later, Jonathan Sir offered me a job. He knew that I was from a very poor family and could not afford to be a volunteer.'

'What happened to your younger brother?'

Without any hesitation or embarrassment, she explained.

'He had a terrible fear of dirt. We first noticed it when he was thirteen. He began washing his hands every few minutes. Then things became so bad that he scrubbed his hands till they were bloody. The village doctor said that the illness was in his mind. So I brought him here and Aditya Sir diagnosed him with obsessive compulsive disorder.' Neelima smiled, 'My brother will be graduating this year. He is thinking about joining the civil services.'

'What about his disorder? Is he cured?'

'He's fine. Aditya Sir sees him once every two months and sometimes, he visits Anjana Ma'am for therapy. Things are well under control... Some more coffee, Ma'am?'

'No, thanks,' Deepa said as she pulled a paper from the pile before her. After a long time, she was feeling hopeful.

***

Deepa started visiting Manas regularly. Despite her initial apprehension, the course work posed no problem for her. Her intelligence and empathy made the job easier than she had expected. Then, of course, there was Jonathan, who despite his busy schedule took time out to encourage her.

As she got to know Jonathan, Deepa was amazed. She had rarely seen any person so open and transparent; someone with no hesitation in talking about his own mental illness. Deepa soon got to know the entire story from the bits and pieces that he shared.

Jonathan's mother was diagnosed with manic depression in her late twenties. By then, she was married and was already a mother. Jonathan's father was a quiet and studious man, happy to be with his books and students. His life was unsettled by his wife's diagnosis, but he faced the impediment head on. He treated his wife's manic depression like any other illness and never shied away from discussing it with others. Jonathan's mother had a relatively normal life until a terrible bus accident snuffed out her life.

Life continued after she was gone, till one day Jonathan realised that all was not well with him. He had always been very self-aware because of his mother's mental disorder and he saw the first few symptoms coming. There was irritable anger, sometimes a need to achieve impossible goals and extreme frustration when they did not work out. But what really got his attention was the disappearing incident.

One day, Jonathan simply vanished without his phone, wallet or scooter. When he did not return home at night, his terrified family lodged a police complaint, but there was no trace of him. Two long days and nights later, Jonathan walked into his house as if nothing had happened. The relieved family didn't ask him any questions and the police dropped the case, but it left Jonathan puzzled.

He told Deepa about this one afternoon while having a casual conversation over coffee, 'When I couldn't remember where I had been the past two days, I knew that something was seriously wrong. Immediately, I took an emergency appointment with Aditya.'

'Why did you think of going to a psychiatrist? The two blank days could have been a symptom of anything. It could have been a neurological problem that probably resulted in a temporary loss of memory.'

'Yes, it could have been. But I thought that I must check with a psychiatrist first because of my mother. Did I ever mention to you that she was manic depressive?'

Deepa marvelled at his openness and frank answers. Would she ever be able to talk honestly about her husband and son?

'You must be on strong medication. How do you manage working here and at your college in the evenings? How did you deal with it all in the beginning?'

'First, I had an honest discussion with Aditya. He said that it was possible to completely suppress the manic and depressive behaviour through prescription drugs, but that it would also make me have, as Kay Jamison once said, "a stunningly boring life". Have you heard of Kay Redfield Jamison?'

Deepa shook her head.

'She's an American clinical psychologist and one of the best there is, but she candidly talks about her own battles with bipolar disorder. I should give you one of her inspiring books to read.'

'But how can you lead a normal life when you have a mental disorder? It is so sinister.'

'It's not sinister; it's a disorder, Deepa. The best part is that most cases are treatable. These days, doctors carefully monitor the dosage so as to discipline the disorder, but not to let the person become non-functional. By the way, do you know that many famous people with very demanding public responsibilities had depression? Churchill was one of them.'

'Churchill? Do you mean Sir Winston Churchill?' she asked in disbelief.

'Yes, so were Leo Tolstoy, Charles Dickens, William Faulkner and Claude Monet. Coming to bipolar disorder, the most famous name that comes to mind is Florence Nightingale, while other names include Ernest Hemingway and actors Mel Gibson and Linda Hamilton.'

Deepa's mouth was agape, as Jonathan's had once been, when Aditya had shared this trivia with him. Despite all the research available on the Internet, this piece of information had escaped her.

Jonathan did not know that the words coming from a person enduring a mental disorder were much more effective on Deepa than all the compassion and assurances given by a psychiatrist or a psychologist. She was beginning to feel hopeful about Raj leading a normal life.

15

Months went by and soon it was November, time for Aditya's three-day seminar in Kolkata. He was really looking forward to the seminar but hated the prospect of packing for the trip. Somehow, he made himself to pull out his travel bag from the closet and got down to the chore.

Halfway into it, his phone rang. Aditya paused and looked at the number. He was surprised to see that it was Smita, Jayant's wife.

'Hi, Smita.'

'Aditya, am I disturbing you?'

'No.' He paused. 'Please tell me.'

'I heard that you are travelling to Kolkata.'

Aditya was intrigued. How did news travel so fast?

'Who told you?'

'I met Rekha Aunty at a wedding yesterday. She told me.'

Ah, the gossip mill.

Smita hesitated.

'Since you are going to Kolkata, can I ask you for a favour?'

'Of course. Do you want me to get something from there?'

'Oh no, I don't need anything. I only want to send something for my parents.'

Her father's nihilistic delusion and the family's denial came to Aditya's mind and he was miffed for a moment.

Smita continued:

'I need to send some Ayurvedic medicines for my father's sinus problem and my mother's gout treatment. This time, the doctor has given a small bottle of massage oil for my mother, along with the usual pills. The couriers are refusing to take the oil. Can you please take the packet with you?'

He tried to wriggle out of it.

'I don't mind carrying the medicines, but I am not going to the city. My seminar is at a resort in the outskirts and I will go there directly from the airport.'

'I know about that. My parents live right next to the airport.'

'No problem then.' Aditya had no choice and gave in. 'But I won't have time to stop on my way to the resort. I can only make the delivery on my way back to the airport. Is it alright if there is a three-day delay?'

'Absolutely no problems. Thank you so much.' Smita was happy.

'How's your father doing?'

'Baba is fine. He is very busy. It is exam time for him.'

Aditya was referring to her father's health and Smita had tactfully sidestepped his question. He decided to be direct. 'Is he seeing a psychiatrist?'

'I don't know,' she said smoothly. 'I'm sure that my mother is taking care of things.'

How could she not know? Smita was quite close to her parents and this was such an important matter. Anyway, beyond a point it was none of his business. Aditya returned to the reason for the call.

'Would you like me to send someone to pick up the medicine from you?'

'No, no. Someone will drop the package at your place.'

'Perfect. Bye.'

Aditya grimaced as she hung up.

***

Aditya planned his last day in Kolkata in a way that he could drop by Smita's parents' house to deliver the medicines, have a cup of tea and then leave for the airport. But when he called the old couple, they insisted that he come to lunch with them. Aditya did have a few hours before his flight and he agreed to come by. In a way, he was also curious to see how Smita's father was faring after all this time.

When Aditya reached Smita's parents' home, they laid out a big spread for him. There were three varieties of fish, a delicious mutton curry, fried brinjals and *daal* with rice; all cooked the traditional Bengali way. Then came the dessert – *mishtidoi* and *sandesh*. Throughout the lunch, the conversation at the dining table was warm and jovial. Aditya relished the meal and enjoyed his hosts' company. He was relieved; there was seemingly nothing abnormal about Smita's father.

Lunch over, Smita's mother stayed back in the kitchen with the part-time maid while the two men moved to the living room. As soon as Aditya was comfortably seated, Smita's father said in a low voice:

'I want to ask you something.'

'What is it, Uncle?'

'How are Jayant and Smita these days?'

'They are fine, Uncle,' he replied.

'I worry a lot for them. I need to know whether they are mentally prepared.'

'For what?'

'About the possibility of losing their son.'

Aditya felt a chill run down his spine. Was Litu unwell? Smita or Jayant hadn't said a word to him.

'What happened, Uncle?'

Smita's father was taken aback.

'Oh, don't you know? Litu is on his deathbed. I don't know what the exact problem is, but I am waiting patiently. I will meet him soon.'

Aditya looked at him with dismay.

'My heart breaks every time I think of my daughter and her husband. It is not going to be easy for them after Litu dies. They'll need a lot of support and counselling. I wish I could be of some help,' he sighed.

Seconds later, the cheerfulness returned.

'You know, Aditya, it may sound morbid, but I am looking forward to meeting Litu and having him stay with us. My wife and I have had such a lonely life after our death.'

'But Uncle, you are very much alive…'

'People don't know that we are wandering souls. I haven't told anyone.' He winked. 'There are only three people in the world who know the truth – Smita, Jayant and you.'

Smita's mother walked into the room and the conversation instantly stopped. It was also time for Aditya to leave. He said goodbye to his hosts and got into the waiting taxi. He was perturbed. Should he have talked to Smita's mother before leaving?

Fifteen minutes later, as he was entering the airport, he picked up his phone and made a call.

'Hi Jayant, I've just delivered the medicines to Smita's parents.'

'Great. I'll tell Smita. I hope you are bringing back some *sandesh* for us.'

Aditya got really irritated. Couldn't the man think of anything apart from food?

'Has Litu been sick, Jayant?'

The line went quiet for a few seconds.

'Why? What did Smita's father say to you?' said Jayant.

'He said that Litu is critically ill.'

'God! Why doesn't he understand? We have been reasoning with him for days, but he's convinced that we are trying to hide something from him. Litu is absolutely fine, Aditya. He had stomach flu six months ago, but he hasn't fallen sick after that – not even a common cold or a fever. But my father-in-law just doesn't believe us.'

'This isn't something that you can control, Jayant. It's his disorder.'

'Oh no! Is it the delusion again?' He sounded alarmed.

'Yes, it is. He might snap out of it like he did the last time, but he definitely needs to see a psychiatrist right away. This is not a good sign.' Aditya was emphatic. 'He needs to be treated. He really, really needs help.'

'I'll tell Smita to have a frank conversation with her mother and persuade her to take my father-in-law to a psychiatrist.'

On that note, Aditya said his goodbye and disconnected the call. He realised that he could do nothing more. He hoped that the family would recognise the gravity of the situation and take action, the way Deepa had.

Despite her hesitation and uncertainty, Deepa started taking Raj to the therapist. Aditya knew that the entire process was more of a struggle for her than for her son. Things changed when she began volunteering in Jonathan's organisation and got the opportunity to observe Anjana Singh's work. Soon, her apprehensions withered away and a new respect for Anjana took its place.

Over time, Aditya noticed a gradual change in Deepa. She was easing up and realising that there were people in the world who were going through much more hardship than what she had once been subjected to or was going through now.

One day, she talked to Aditya about it.

'How do people deal with the stigma?' she asked. 'The person suffering from mental illness may not even notice the change in other people's behaviour towards them, but it's tough for their family and close friends.'

'I agree, it is very hard to be the subject of people's judgemental comments and their stares. Our society must change for things to get better.

In the west, people talk about seeing a therapist without discomfort, but in India, people won't even go to one unless the situation became unmanageable. And even when they start seeing one, they don't like to talk about it.'

'But isn't that wrong? Jonathan talks about his bipolar disorder as if it is like a persistent knee problem or something like that.'

'I know. That's the right approach. Hopefully, our society will evolve and things will change in time... By the way, how's work?'

Deepa had finished her training followed by the three-month apprenticeship. Now, she was one of the regular volunteers at Manas.

'I love it,' she replied. 'It's a privilege to work with Jonathan. He's such a brilliant and dedicated man. We need more people like him in this world.' Her admiration was sincere.

'And how is Raj taking to Anjana? Has he become comfortable with her?'

'Yes, he has. I'm so glad that you referred Raj to her. She's so easy to talk to,' she said as she stood up to leave.

Aditya knew that a good therapist could work wonders with Raj, but it could take weeks or months before there were any noticeable results.

'Take care, Deepa,' he said. 'Bring Raj for his next appointment after two months.'

'I will. Bye, Aditya!'

***

A couple of months later, Deepa and Raj came to meet Aditya in his clinic.

'You look good,' Aditya greeted her.

She smiled self-consciously.

'Thanks. I have lost about four kilos, but I have a long way to go.'

'I'm not talking about your weight...' Aditya stopped himself. He was seeing the girl he remembered from his college days – always smiling and cheerful. Volunteering at Jonathan's organisation was definitely doing her some good.

When Raj was waiting in the reception at the end of the appointment, Aditya called Deepa inside his room.

'Tell me, how do you think Raj is doing at his sessions with the therapist?' he asked.

'I think it is probably working.'

'Be patient, Deepa. These things take time.'

'I know. I'll wait for as long as I have to.'

***

Time moved on and Anjana reduced Raj's sessions from twice a week to once a week. A year later, it was again reduced to once in two weeks with the understanding that it could go down further.

Deepa called Aditya to give him the good news about Raj's revised schedule with Anjana.

'I'm so glad that things are looking up. This calls for a celebration,' Aditya said.

'Absolutely.' She thought for a moment and said, 'Why don't we meet for dinner? When can you and your wife come home? I make the finest mutton cutlets and the best trifle pudding in town.'

'But…' he tried to interrupt.

'Do you mind if I invite Anjana too? That reminds me, Prakash is planning to come to Bangalore next weekend. We can plan it that time.'

'I was joking about the celebration, Deepa,' Aditya said. 'Actually we can't come over this weekend or even the next. I'm going for an international conference at the end of the week. After that, Prachi and I plan to take a vacation. Mutton cutlets and trifle pudding sound delicious but they'll have to wait till the end of December or early January. Would you mind if I take a rain check?'

'Not at all!' Deepa said, though she was clearly disappointed.

***

The conference in Kuala Lumpur and the vacation weren't excuses. In fact, Aditya and Prachi planned to escape to the Langkawi islands for a quiet vacation right after the conference.

Usually, whenever Aditya went out of town, he always shared his files with Dr Raghu Banerjee, who saw his patients in case of an emergency. He and Dr Banerjee had worked together earlier.

Aditya sat down to go through the case files systematically to see which ones might need Dr Banerjee's attention while he would be gone. While flipping through the pages of a particular file, thoughtful lines creased his forehead. It was Ali's file. What happened to the man, he wondered. Shabnam was supposed to have come back with her husband to the clinic in two weeks with the test results, but there had been no communication.

Aditya dialled Jonathan's number on an impulse.

'Are you free for a few minutes? I need to talk to you about a case.'

'Sure.'

'Remember Shabnam? You had sent her to me. Her husband Ali is probably suffering from hypersexuality.'

There was a pause.

'Right. Right. I remember,' said Jonathan.

'Well, she was supposed to come back with test reports after a few weeks, but she didn't. Do you know what happened?'

'Let me find out. I'll call you back.'

Three hours later, Jonathan phoned back.

'Sorry, Doctor, I have bad news. Ali refused to go for the tests. He's turned his wife's life into a living hell. He maligned her in the neighbourhood.'

'But why would anyone believe such an immoral and shameless man?'

'I wish I knew. I talked to Shabnam but she does not want to come to our organisation now. Poor woman. She's absolutely distraught.'

Aditya was concerned.

'Can't you do something, Jonathan?'

'I'll try, but it's not going to be easy.'

Aditya kept Ali's file aside. This wasn't going to need Dr Banerjee's attention. He turned to the next file on the heap.

17

The conference in Kuala Lumpur ended on a high note. Aditya's paper was discussed and appreciated by many academicians and researchers, who had gathered from all around the globe. It was followed by the usual gala dinner, which was crowded and noisy, but Aditya and Prachi attended it happily; sometimes it was good from a networking point of view.

Next day, they took the early morning flight to Langkawi from Kuala Lumpur. The drive from the airport to the resort was a short one. The place was serene and well-run; the travel agency had booked them a sea-facing cottage. This cottage was on stilts and had a view straight out of an artist's imagination. The sea was a beautiful, calm blue.

Prachi was ecstatic.

'This is so surreal. I don't want to move from here.'

Aditya agreed, as he lowered himself on the rattan sofa in the wooden balcony. Before he knew it, he had dozed off into a lovely, restful sleep.

***

After a couple of days, they realised that they had seen all there was to the resort.

'I think we should step out of the resort and go see the island.'

'Sure. The travel desk was selling me a great deal on a new-model Mercedes for hire. Let's take that.'

Prachi felt no fascination for the Mercedes; all she wanted was a drive to see the natural beauty of the place.

'I was talking to the concierge in the morning. He says that the best place to watch the sunset is a beach near the museum. Want to go?'

'Of course!' *Here I come, dear Mercedes*. Aditya felt the exhilaration of a schoolboy.

The beach was a good twenty minutes' drive, but the best part was there weren't any tourists. They sat down on the fine, white sand, quite mesmerised, as the sun moved down languidly, finally disappearing behind a small hill on some distant island. They soaked in the soft twilight and only when it started getting dark did they get up to leave.

As he drove back up the winding road, Aditya started humming to himself.

'Do you know how Langkawi got its name?' Prachi asked.

'No. No idea.'

'Lang is a short form of *helang*. *Helang* means eagle. *Kawi* means reddish brown. So Langkawi means reddish brown eagle.'

'That is neither romantic nor interesting. Kind of lame.'

'Okay, you want to know more interesting things. Let me tell you one… There was this beautiful woman called Mahsuri. She was happily married but became good friends with a travelling musician while her husband was away fighting a battle. Her in-laws and, later on, the entire village accused her of adultery. They said she must die. But no sword could kill her. Finally it was Mahsuri who got her own sword and when she was killed, white blood came out and then everyone realised she was innocent. As she died, she cursed the island that for seven generations it would have no peace and prosperity.'

'Now, that is a gloomy story.' Aditya made a face.

'Maybe. But the good thing is the seven generations are past now. The island has become prosperous once again.'

Aditya looked at Prachi incredulously.

'How do you know? It is just a story.'

'Well, the adultery and curse part may be something of folklore. But there actually was a beautiful woman called Mahsuri who was killed. Believe me, there are ancient paintings to corroborate this. After she died, her husband and son went away to Thailand. Surprisingly, Langkawi became a battlefield, a lot of political unrest followed. You may say it was just a coincidence. But the fact remains there is a seventh-generation descendant of Mahsuri who lives in Phuket in Thailand.'

'How do you know all this?' Aditya asked again.

'The Internet. How else? When you were busy giving final touches to your paper in Kuala Lumpur, I was surfing the Net. Trying to find out the best places to see, to shop and to eat. I have my notes all here.' Prachi waved a small diary.

'That's nice. So tell me a nice place for Thai food. After all the satays in the last few days, I want a change.'

'Thai?' Prachi opened her diary. 'Here we go…'

When they arrived, they found the place quaint and very romantic. They chose a table outside. The soft breeze and a melodious Thai tune playing on the music system were just perfect. But the restaurant did not have an English menu. Everything was written in Malay, Thai and Chinese. Thankfully, the owner spoke broken English. With a little struggle and some help from him, Prachi decided what they were going to order. A nutmeg and pumpkin soup with an arugula and pine nut salad. The main course was going to be chicken with figs and almonds.

***

While Prachi did the ordering, Aditya was watching her. He loved her animated manner; she looked so charming. The owner left with the order.

Prachi realised that Aditya was looking at her.

'What?'

'Nothing.' Aditya was smiling.

'Why are you smiling, then?'

'Do you realise something? All the foods you just ordered are considered aphrodisiacs.'

'Come on!'

'You don't believe me? Just wait and see what happens.'

'Will you stop now? Can't you talk about anything else?' Prachi looked at him with disapproval.

'What did I do?' Aditya said very innocently. 'You're the one who ordered the food.'

The food came after a little wait, served course by course. It was wonderfully delectable.

'This is probably the best Thai food I have ever eaten. Now I must have some ice cream,' Prachi declared.

'Mango, chocolate or vanilla, Ma'am?' The owner asked.

'Vanilla.With hot chocolate sauce.'

Aditya smiled again.

'Now what?' Prachi demanded.

'The scent and flavour of vanilla is believed to increase lust. And you just ordered that.'

Prachi blushed.

'Stop it.'

***

As he got into the car, Aditya glanced at his phone. There were two missed calls. He was puzzled; in the quiet ambience of the Thai restaurant, he should have heard the phone ring. He was sure that it was not family; his mother had called on Prachi's phone just before they stepped into the restaurant to report that all was well. It was probably a wrong number.

Prachi noticed her husband's distraction.

'What happened?'

'There are a couple of missed calls. I am wondering if there is any problem with any patient. Of course, Raghu Banerjee is there…'

'But Raghu is like the last resort. Someone to go to only in an emergency.'

'True.'

'Imagine, if you build an organisation other doctors would be available in the same set up; it would be so nice.'

'You are right. It would be reassuring for the patients. But I don't think I can build something like that.' There was a tinge of regret in his voice.

'Why do you always say that?' Prachi said. 'I wouldn't bring it up over and over again if you were not capable. Give it a thought, at least.'

Aditya looked at Prachi and nodded.

***

The blissful time at Langkawi was coming to an end. It was the last day.

'Let's go island hopping.' Prachi suggested over breakfast. The charm of the blue-green waters had cast its spell on her.

Aditya was quick to agree. Like the fancy rental car, the idea of sailing in a motorboat excited him in a boyish way.

'Langkawi has ninety-nine gorgeous islands though only a few are inhabited. That is why the natural beauty is still intact there.' Prachi started her researched commentary. 'Right, Mahmud?'

The young boat owner with limited English nodded in agreement as he steered the motorboat from the inlet into the waters of the Andaman Sea. He started off slow and it seemed as if the trip was going to be a smooth sail. That definitely was not what Aditya had wanted. To his delight, soon the boat gathered speed. They were whizzing past islands, the saltwater spray and the breeze drenched them. Towards the end, they could clearly see the skyline of Pulau Langkawi. Prachi nudged Aditya. She was saying something, but he could not hear her over the sound of the motorboat.

Mahmud slowed down the boat. Now that he was near the main island, he had to be careful. He had got into trouble on two separate occasions for over-speeding and somehow extricated himself with hefty fines. A third offence would probably see him lose his license; he had no intention of doing that.

'What?' Aditya shouted over the sound of the engine.

'Your phone!' Prachi screamed back at him with a gesture.

Only then was Aditya aware of the phone ringing in his pocket. He took the phone out and stared at it. There was no name or number. Aditya pressed the 'talk' button.

'Aditya?' Aditya was surprised to hear Deepa.

'Deepa? Is everything okay? How is Raj?' Aditya became very alert.

'All well, Aditya. Are you back in Bangalore?' Aditya could barely hear her.

'Not yet. We are still in Malaysia. What happened?'

'Oh no, nothing at all. I assumed you have returned and thought of reminding you about our dinner plans. Sorry for disturbing you on your vacation.'

Somehow, Aditya felt it wasn't just that. There was probably something.

'No problem at all. Why don't I give you a call after reaching Bangalore? I am back on Saturday.'

'Sure, Aditya. Bye. Sorry again.' She hung up.

Prachi looked at him quizzically.

'It was a call from Deepa? What was that about? Anything serious?'

He shrugged.

'No idea. Why would she call me suddenly? She was speaking about the dinner invitation, but who knows? I hope everything is okay.'

'Call her once you reach home.'

'I will.'

18

On reaching Bangalore on Saturday afternoon, Aditya first called Dr Raghu Banerjee. It was good to know that only one of his patients had gone to see him – that too for an allergic reaction to a particular medicine.

Next, he called Deepa.

'Aditya, you are back? I am so sorry I disturbed you on your vacation.'

'No issues. But is everything okay? We were out at sea when you called and the signal was weak; I could barely hear your voice that day… Did you call a couple of times before? There were two missed calls.'

Deepa laughed self-consciously.

'I did… I tried to, but lost my nerve.'

Lost her nerve about what, Aditya wanted to ask, instead he just repeated his earlier question, 'Are things okay?'

'Everything is fine. It is just… just that I want to talk about a few things… I could not wait to tell you.'

'So, tell me.'

'I don't know how,' she faltered. 'Something has changed. I feel hopeful… Do you ever feel that way?'

Aditya was surprised; he was not sure where the conversation was going.

Before he could say anything, Deepa continued:

'Earlier I used to dread the mornings; now I look forward to it. These days I go for long walks and there is this park nearby and it is full of flowers and birds. I have been here almost two years now, but didn't realise that this place can be so magical in winter.'

It was true that Bangalore became very beautiful in December. Winter here was mild, but why was Deepa suddenly discussing the city and the weather with him?

'It just makes me feel happy and I am making up for lost time,' she was gushing.

'That is nice, but what is it that you wanted to talk to me about?' He was careful and very alert.

'It is… it is about us. Our future.'

Aditya almost dropped the phone. There was an uncomfortable feeling and he did not know how to address that. Us? What about us? And what future?

Deepa quickly realised her words; she was mortified. She laughed awkwardly and said, 'I was … I was talking about me and my son – about *our* future.'

Aditya breathed easy.

'I have been having mostly these crazy thoughts…' She said as if to ease the awkwardness, 'I want to speak to you as Raj's doctor and my friend… you could probably help me to make sense of what is going on in my mind.'

'Sure. Come over on Monday to my clinic. Come by nine.'

'I will be there. Thanks, Aditya.'

***

Deepa was on time. She had a spring in her step. Aditya hadn't ever seen her as exuberant as she was now. She was in a blue crepe sari with an embroidered border. Her face glowed and make-up concealed her wrinkles. She wore a pair of sapphire earrings. She looked different – very pretty.

'How is Raj?' Aditya asked.

'Fine. He is such a pleasure to deal with these days. I had no idea that my son was such a caring and affectionate boy.' Her voice dropped. 'Aditya, thanks for everything.'

'I've simply done my duty.'

'No, you've done so much more than that. I have spent decades dealing with doctors, medicines and therapy. I know the difference between treatment and compassionate care. I pray that you are always able to treat your patients with such sensitivity.' There was a deep sense of gratitude and sincerity in her words.

'Thanks, Deepa,' Aditya smiled. 'And what's the latest from Bobby?'

'Bobby who?' She laughed, 'He's vanished into thin air. Raj doesn't talk about him.'

She continued:

'I wanted to ask you… do you think that I can go back to London with Raj?'

'London?'

'I know it creates its own uncertainty, but I'm finding it extremely difficult to ignore my life, my feelings. When things became overwhelming, I simply locked my house and came away to Bangalore. Since then, I've been missing my house and my personal life.'

'Will you be able to manage on your own?' Aditya wondered.

'I won't be alone…' Deepa spoke slowly. 'I don't think I have ever told you about Ethan, have I?'

'No, but I've read about him in your journal.'

'Ethan was my colleague. When life became hell, he was the one who stood by my side. He's always been there for me.'

But wasn't all that before Raj became very sick, Aditya pondered.

'I am in a relationship with him. In fact, Ethan proposed marriage a year after Naren's death. I knew that if there was anyone who could accept Raj whole-heartedly, it was he. But life had other plans. You would have read about Ethan's ski accident and the slow, painful recovery. We had to postpone our wedding date to five months later. I noticed Raj's behavioural changes during those months. And after that…'

'Ethan broke off with you.' Aditya completed her sentence.

'What are you talking about?' Deepa sounded surprised.

'Isn't that why you came away from London?'

'No, no. The truth is that I really don't know why. After Raj's problem started, I found myself on the verge of a nervous breakdown. I was confused and upset and I didn't want to burden Ethan with my issues.'

When the doctors had finally given Ethan a clean chit, he had immediately wanted to discuss their wedding. But she wasn't enthusiastic any more. She told him about Raj. Ethan became quite worried and wanted her to consult a psychiatrist, but Deepa was reluctant. Her husband's treatment was still fresh in her mind and she wanted a break. She wanted to leave London and go to Bangalore, where her father had a small house.

'Ethan wanted to take charge of Raj's life; it was me who ran away. But, he didn't give up and stayed in touch. It was I who felt aloof. Now that my son is better, I find myself constantly thinking of Ethan. I miss him... and my home and garden. It must be in shambles by now. I have to put it back in order... put my life back in order.'

Aditya was listening intently.

'Can we move back to London? Is Raj doing well enough to relocate?' she asked nervously.

'Of course, he can go. You should get back to your normal life too. It'll be good for you and for Raj. But Deepa, you must remember that Raj will need to be constantly monitored.'

'I know,' she nodded. 'But Aditya, if you come to London, don't forget to meet me. I will introduce you to Ethan. I think that you will like each other.'

'When are you planning to leave?'

'Not right away – maybe in four to six months. Anjana thinks that Raj may not require the frequent therapy sessions after March; maybe only once a month.'

'That's good.' Aditya was glad.

'I feel bad about leaving Manas, but Jonathan introduced me to a British organisation associated with Manas and they have shown interest. I'm glad when I go to London, I don't have to look for some other kind of job. This will be much more satisfying.'

'True.'

She was ready to leave.

'Aditya, I'll let you know once the date is finalised.'

'Thanks. Meanwhile, keep sending Raj to me for regular check-ups. Getting back to London now would not be without its challenges. Are you sure you can handle that?'

'Of course. Ethan will be with me and I'm sure that we can manage things together. Oh, I almost forgot. When are you and your wife free for dinner?'

'When do you want us to come?'

'Saturday?' Deepa queried.

'I think that should be alright. I'll talk to Prachi and send you a text message.'

'Oh, good. Bye, Aditya.'

As Aditya watched her go, he hoped that things would work out for her. Life had been rough on her and she deserved to find happiness.

19

Soon, the days became hectic. The morning appointments at the clinic were completely full and Aditya barely had time to update the case files even as his afternoon round of appointments began. Prachi also got very busy catching up with work at the hospital and invariably returned home exhausted.

The frenzied routine continued till the end of January. Then came February, which brought spring and a somewhat slower pace for Aditya.

'Let's go out for lunch today,' Prachi said while they were having breakfast together on a beautiful Wednesday morning.

'Today is a working day, my dear.' Aditya reminded her.

'So what? We doctors also need to take care of our emotional health and bond with our loved ones.'

'How about dinner, then?' Aditya queried.

'No, not dinner. We'll be so tired by the end of the day that we won't feel like going out.'

'But don't you have to be in the hospital all day?'

'I'll manage a couple of hours off in the afternoon. And you'll have to do just that,' she insisted.

Sometimes, Prachi could be impulsive and Aditya loved her spontaneity.

'Okay, that sounds nice.' He ruffled her hair.

'We should do this more often. I have heard that couples in the west have a "date night" every week to keep romance alive in their marriage. Maybe we should have our own weekly "date lunch".'

'Sure. Why not?' Aditya added with a straight face, 'But date nights culminate in interesting things. Do you think a "date lunch" could also be like that?'

'Shut up.' Prachi blushed with a furtive glance at the kitchen where the cleaning lady was pottering around, 'You really cross the line sometimes.'

'Sorry, sorry,' he said without a trace of apology on his face. 'Where do you want to go for lunch?'

'Well, my colleagues have been raving about a new Italian restaurant called "Olives and Cheese". It is quite near your clinic. Let's eat there.'

'Sure. I'll ask Aruna to make the reservation. Come to my clinic at one and pick me up. There's no point in taking two cars.'

'I'll do that.' She felt energised and went into the bedroom to get ready. A minute later, she called out to Aditya, 'What should I wear today?'

Ah, the eternal question.

'How about the new red sari that you bought the other day?' he responded.

'My God, that sari? No way. I can't wear slinky red chiffon to the hospital. What about the pink sari with the subtle white embroidery– the one that you helped me choose in the quaint little designer shop in Connaught Place in Delhi?'

Aditya always had shopping amnesia. He did not ever remember picking out a sari – pink or any other colour, but he was not going to get engaged in a conversation about saris. Quickly, he agreed, 'Yes, yes! The pink sari would be lovely.'

***

The pasta and salad were delicious at "Olives and Cheese". Their ingredients were fresh and some of the spices were clearly imported. As they were about to finish off the lunch with tiramisu, Prachi's phone rang.

It was the receptionist from the hospital.

'Yes, Prabha?' asked Prachi. She listened intently and said, 'Okay, I'll be there as soon as I can.' After disconnecting the call, Prachi looked at her husband seriously, 'We need to leave.'

'Sure. What's the problem?'

'I'll tell you later. First, let me see how things are at the hospital.'

Aditya quickly settled the bill without a word and the couple walked back to their car. As Prachi started the car, she pressed her one-touch button to call the hospital and moved to the hands-free mode. She drove as she spoke to the duty doctor and continued to give him instructions. After dropping Aditya at the clinic, she simply drove away without a proper goodbye.

That evening, Aditya returned home earlier than usual. It was Prachi who was always there by the time he came home since her hospital was nearer to their house. But today, her car was not in the driveway. He looked at his phone; there was no message or phone call. Maybe she was late because of the emergency case today.

Aditya showered, changed and made himself a cup of tea. Then he saw her text message. 'I will be late. Should be back by ten.'

That meant he had two more hours to kill. What was he going to do by himself? Aditya disliked watching television, so that was not an option. He thought about going to his study and reading a book, but he was really tired and did not feel like doing anything mentally stimulating. Soon, Aditya found himself pacing– something that he rarely did.

Why was the house so quiet?

If only they had a child, he thought, things would have been different today. The house would not have been so forlorn… he would not have been so lonely. The thought startled him.

After his break up with Deepa, it had taken years for Aditya to move on and when he finally met Prachi and they married, he was keen to start a family. She, too, was very fond of children and wanted to be a mother soon after their marriage; but she could not conceive. When they got themselves checked, it turned out that Prachi had a tubal blockage. They didn't give up. They consulted many gynaecologists and sent Prachi's reports to doctors overseas.

Unfortunately, all of them came to almost the same conclusion. With a complete blockage of the fallopian tubes, conception was going to be difficult without intervention. The treatment involved surgery – it would be physically uncomfortable, time-consuming, expensive, and might cause unpleasant side-effects, they were told. Moreover, there was no guarantee of success.

Prachi and Aditya talked about it for months and in the end, they decided not to opt for a complicated surgery with an uncertain outcome. They also discussed adoption, but somehow could not make up their minds. Finally, they decided to leave things as they were. They had each other and they had careers that they loved. That would have to be enough for this lifetime.

But if a baby had come within the first couple of years, then the child would have been twelve years old now. Would it have been a boy or a girl? What would the child look like? Prachi's skin and his features? Or the other way round? And what would he be – Papa, Baba or Dad?

His feelings took him by surprise. It was an emotion he was careful not to go near, but on rare occasions, it caught hold of him. Like today.

Aditya stopped pacing and sat down. He picked up a news magazine and tried to concentrate. He should not let his mind do the what-ifs. It would only pull him into a downward spiral. How did Prachi handle it? As a woman, her maternal instinct was obviously much stronger than his. Did working with children every day make it worse, or did it help her in some way?

The door opened and Prachi walked in. She looked very tired. The pink sari was limp and there was no trace of the glow that had lit up her face in the morning. She noticed Aditya's empty teacup and asked, 'Why haven't you had dinner yet? It's so late!'

'I wasn't hungry. So I thought we'd eat together.'

'Okay, let me have a quick shower first.'

They ate dinner in silence. Just as Aditya was about to pick up the dishes from the dining table, Prachi stopped him, 'Leave them here. We'll do it later. I need to talk to you.'

She made two cups of hot chocolate and they settled down in the courtyard.

'Aditya, is it possible for a young child to have a mental disorder?' Prachi asked without preamble. She added, 'I am not talking about retardation.'

He nodded.

'It is possible. You know Deepa's son was diagnosed with schizophrenia.'

'No, no, I am not talking about teenagers. What about a nine- or ten-year-old boy? Is it possible for a child to have depression at such a young age?'

'Hmm, it isn't impossible. But why do you ask?'

'You know that phone call at lunch? Well, I've been seeing this patient – a boy – for about two years now.

The parents insist that he is very mischievous and therefore, quite accident-prone. This child has already been saved once from certain death. That time he jumped from his first-floor terrace. Fortunately, he fell on a big mango tree beside their house and got caught in the branches before he crashed to the ground. He had multiple fractures and a broken nose, but there was no internal bleeding or anything more serious. He was hospitalised for some time. At the time, I assumed that he was doing a superhero and that he would be careful after that fall.'

Prachi had reason to believe the superhero story. Many accidents involved young children, who thought they could fly like Superman or, like Spiderman, could climb up tall buildings.

'What happened now?' Aditya asked as he took a sip of the hot chocolate.

'While I was at lunch with you, the boy was brought to the hospital in critical condition. Apparently, when the parents were at work and the maid had gone to the market, the boy lit a circle of fire in their small backyard and sat down in the centre. Luckily, the neighbour smelt something burning and rescued the child. He was brought to the hospital with forty percent burns. He is critical; I don't know if he will pull through.'

'Did you talk to his parents?'

'I did. The family is middle class, the parents are hard-working people. They are very disturbed and feel terribly guilty. They believe that their son is having near-fatal accidents since both of them work. But I don't think that that's the case; I have a strong suspicion that he's doing all this on purpose.'

'That's quite a serious allegation, Prachi.'

'I know. That's why I wanted to speak to you before giving my opinion. What do you think?' She looked at him.

'I can't say for certain without knowing more details. If your instincts are telling you that the boy may be suffering from a psychological disorder, then there may be some truth to it and you must investigate.'

'But I can't take this further until I know, Aditya. Could a ten year old have such severe depression that he would attempt suicide?'

'It's possible, Prachi. Years ago, doctors thought that depression, bipolarity and other mental disorders were purely adult ailments and that children don't get them. So doctors believed that an accident was the result of the child's stupidity. Children love to imitate; sometimes such incidents were attributed to "copy-cat" behaviour. But things are changing now. Psychiatrists agree that a pre-adolescent child can suffer from depression due to various reasons.'

'But isn't ten a little too young for...?'

Aditya interrupted her before she could complete her question.

'I know it is disturbing, but it can happen. And diagnosis is only the first battle of the war. Most parents remain in denial while others delay treatment due to the stigma. Then there are those who argue their child's depression will heal with time.'

'Does it ever?' She was inquisitive.

'It could, if the depression is because of an external factor. But medical intervention is needed. If that is delayed or denied, then the problem can aggravate and move to the chronic stage. That's when it becomes difficult to treat.'

'What's the course of treatment for a child?'

'It's the same as in adults; the child needs anti-depressants.'

Prachi stared at the night sky and then at him, somehow disliking the idea.

'That's the only known treatment in the world today and of course, the dosage is mild,' Aditya added. 'It is extremely important to start the child on anti-depressants right away, because he can hurt himself badly.'

'Yes, I think that's the case with this boy. I'll talk to the Head of Department tomorrow morning and recommend that the child be seen by a psychiatrist after his recovery.'

'I can give you a few names, if you want,' Aditya tried to be helpful.

'Won't you see him?'

'I could, but it's better if he goes to a child psychiatrist.'

Prachi looked despondent.

'If you had a larger set-up, you would have had a child psychiatrist in your office and we would have been able to monitor the boy's progress ourselves.'

Why was she always pushing him to a 'larger set up'? Aditya sighed.

'Don't worry. I'll refer him to someone really good.'

'Would you?' Prachi's concern and distress was beyond a doctor's.

Aditya looked at her intently.

She looked away and then she spoke haltingly, 'This boy is special to me. He resembles you and reminds me of your childhood photograph – the one that your mother keeps in her bedroom. I think that if we had had a child, he would have looked like this boy.'

Deepa and Raj had moved to London in June. It was only towards the end of August that there was a long and cheerful email from Deepa.

Aditya,

I don't know why I ran away from Ethan and my home. When Raj and I reached London, Ethan was waiting for us at the airport. That's when I realised that nothing had changed. When we reached home, my garden was looking glorious. Ethan had been taking care of the house and the garden; he knew how much it would mean to me.

Raj has joined a good public school. The Principal is aware of his condition and has assured me that the school will be supportive. Raj likes both his new psychiatrist and therapist. I hope that he develops good relationships with them, like he had with Anjana and you.

Meanwhile, I have joined the organisation recommended by Jonathan and I am happy.

Ethan and I are planning to get married next summer, possibly in June.

Why don't Prachi and you plan a trip to London around June? It would be lovely to have both of you here for my special day.

Best,

Deepa

Aditya smiled as he typed out a reply. London in June was a great idea, but it would not work for him. He had other commitments during the months of June and July and getting out of those was not going to be possible. However, Prachi and he were thinking of a European vacation the year after next and they would definitely love to meet Deepa, Ethan and Raj.

***

Deepa periodically wrote to him. The update was usually routine – things were going smoothly, Raj was doing fine at school and how Deepa's work was tedious but satisfying. Ethan was a stabilising factor in her life, cheerfully sharing the responsibilities of the house and keeping the mother and son swathed in a blanket of security. She would let Aditya know about the wedding date once it was finalised.

That email never came. But Aditya wasn't worried – it was a second marriage for both Ethan and Deepa and they must have decided to keep it simple and low-key. Somehow, he also became lax in writing to her.

Another year passed by and it was August again.

***

The last appointment of the day – one that Aditya was really looking forward to – was with Jonathan. As usual, he arrived on the dot.

'Hi, Doc,' Jonathan said cheerfully as he sauntered into his office and handed Aditya his latest blood report.

'Hello, Prof, you're looking good,' remarked Aditya.

'Thanks.'

Jonathan was one of Aditya's ideal patients who took his medicines regularly to ensure that his bipolar disorder was kept in check. Even when he was keeping fine, he would come for his scheduled appointments with the doctor, not wanting to leave anything to chance.

Aditya peered over the report and smiled.

'Everything's in order.'

'When will it be that I wouldn't need my meds anymore?'

'I wish I could tell you to do that.'

'It's very tiring, Doc. Sometimes, just the idea of taking these personality-altering medications all my life distresses me.' Jonathan became serious.

'Stop thinking of the medication as personality altering. Why don't you think of it as an aid that helps you stay on track?' Aditya responded.

'I counsel people who come to Manas saying just that, but things are so different when it concerns your own self. It is good to know that there is a place for me where I can pour out my own misgivings. It is cathartic. I hope you don't mind.'

'Not at all. How are things back at the organisation?'

'Not bad, but it's not going the way I thought it would.'

'What do you mean?'

'I feel extremely frustrated at times.' Jonathan had good reason to feel that way. His organisation regularly sent patients to psychiatrists after counselling. Often, after getting the prescription, the patients changed their minds and never showed up again. The initial feeling of well-being and sometimes the potential stigma prevented them from continuing the treatment.

'We get a lot of people from the poorer section of society and it is very difficult to rid them of superstitions and shame,' he concluded.

As he listened, Aditya's mind went back to Smita and her mother. According to Jayant, the mother–daughter duo had recently resorted to religious rituals to deal with the old man's neuro-psychiatric disorder.

'Actually, it has nothing to do with being poor or rich or educated. Superstition is everywhere,' he said.

'You are right. But can't doctors like you do something? Can't you ensure patients continue their course of treatment?'

Aditya shrugged.

'We are doctors, not cops. We can't force anybody, Jonathan.'

'I wish there was some way of monitoring these cases and making the patients feel that there are people out there who care for them. Maybe it would have been possible had we all been part of a bigger establishment.'

'Then you would be lost in the bureaucracy. It would not be your organisation any longer.'

'Who cares?' Jonathan said intensely. 'I didn't start the organisation for laurels and recognition for myself. It isn't a stepping-stone to fulfil a bigger ambition. I don't mind merging if the patients receive greater benefits. What do you think, Doc?'

'About what?'

'What if we joined hands and had an organisation that specialises in mental health and provides complete patient care, all under one roof? I'm sure that Anjana and the other therapists would also welcome the idea of building a self-sufficient organisation with like-minded doctors.'

'No, that's not my cup of tea.'

Jonathan continued almost as if he hadn't heard him.

'It'll give me something to focus on that's bigger than my organisation and myself. Just imagine – we could have counselling, therapy and medical advice in one place. And a diagnostic lab too. It would be so much easier for the patient and the caregiver, and for us too.'

'It is not an easy proposition.'

'I know. That's why the thought makes me feel dejected. I feel like I am leaving my patients halfway.'

'Please don't think like that, Jonathan. I'm there for you. I'll do all that I can to help you.'

Jonathan laughed.

'Well, I really need your help right now.'

Aditya looked at him questioningly.

'I've given my car for servicing. Since I am your last appointment for the day, will you give me a ride on your way home?'

'Absolutely.'

Jonathan continued the discussion in the car, talking animatedly about several possibilities and different combinations of facilities, but Aditya remained non-committal. Finally, Jonathan prodded him:

'Why are you hesitant? Don't you think it would be fantastic to have such a unique institution in Bangalore?'

'Yes, in a utopian world, it would be wonderful,' Aditya replied. 'But things don't happen that way in reality.'

'What's so utopian about my idea? It's plain and simple common sense.' Jonathan stopped himself. The last thing he wanted was a war of words with his friend.

Aditya did not respond.

A minute later, Jonathan touched Aditya's hand lightly and smiled, 'Ah, here we are. You can drop me right here, Doc.'

'No, I'm dropping you outside your home.'

'But it's out of the way.'

'It doesn't matter. I'm quite sure that I can bear your company for a few more minutes,' Aditya said with a smile. As he turned left into a busy road, Jonathan asked, 'What's the latest from Deepa?'

'She must be alright. The last I heard from her was around a year ago when she wrote to me and said that she was enjoying her new job.'

'Oh, good.' Jonathan nodded, satisfied. 'How is her son? Is the schizophrenia under control?'

Aditya looked at him, surprised, 'How did you know?' He had never discussed Raj with Jonathan.

'Deepa told me about it a few days before she left.'

That was a huge improvement. She had been reluctant to discuss her son with anyone. Jonathan's openness must have rubbed off on her.

'Raj was doing well and must have settled down in his new school by now. And...' He hesitated for a second, unsure of whether to let Jonathan know about Ethan and then decided to tell him, '…she must have gotten married too. She was engaged to a British guy.'

'Oh, really?' Jonathan was genuinely delighted. 'Please give her my heartiest congratulations and best wishes when you write to her.'

'I will.' Aditya made a mental note to send an email to Deepa that night.

***

The email bounced. That was surprising, unless, of course, Deepa had changed her email id. In that case, she should have let him know about it. He thought about contacting Prakash but remembered that he had relocated to South Africa just months after Deepa had moved to London. Prakash wasn't in touch and his last email id would be invalid now. There was nothing Aditya could do but wait for Deepa to get in touch with him.

21

September passed and soon, it was October. October made Aditya nostalgic. The city of Cuttack, where Aditya was born and raised, every year eagerly awaited the season of Dussehra and Kali Puja around this time. There was excitement, revelry and a general sense of well-being that touched everyone. As a child, Aditya used to love the merrymaking, but as he grew older and stepped into his teens, he looked at some of it as crude and stupid. Not for long, though. When he left home and joined medical college, his perspective changed. He understood that the celebrations weren't just for religious reasons – it was a time for everyone to come together, to de-stress, to be happy.

Once he began working, he longed for the festivities even more and managed to take his vacation during Durga Puja. Then he started his private practice in Bangalore, which did not leave him with any time to himself. There was always a yearning to go 'home' to Cuttack in October, but the visit rarely materialised.

That was why Prachi and he were delighted when a group of Bengali friends invited them to celebrate Bijoya, a celebration of the victory of Goddess Durga over the demon Mahisasura after an epic ten-day long battle.

'Shall we go now, Aditya?' said Prachi as she entered his study looking resplendent in a beige-and-red Sambalpuri sari.

'Wow!'

Prachi was flattered.

'Your mother sent this sari for the Puja.'

'Very nice.'

'You also look good.' She had forced her husband to wear a blue tussar silk *kurta* and a white *churidar*.

Aditya made a face.

'Hmmm, I'll manage to get through tonight but these clothes are very uncomfortable.'

'You crib too much. Let's go.' As she turned around, she realised that her husband was staring at his laptop, 'What are you doing? Don't tell me that you are checking emails again.'

'Why don't you start the car? I'll join you in just a minute,' he scrolled down his inbox.

Aditya had submitted a paper to the Psychiatric Research Society for their upcoming conference in

Australia but had not received a reply for several weeks now. It was unusual for them to take this long, he thought pensively as he began shutting down his laptop. This particular paper was close to his heart because it was about teenage depression. His discussions in forums and conferences had been highly appreciated, which had prompted him to research the subject. The final outcome of his research was the article that he had sent to the Society for evaluation. How long were they going to make him wait? Aditya thought irritably as he joined Prachi.

***

The first people they met at the Bijoya celebrations were Jayant and Smita, who had also been invited. Smita rushed over to them.

'I'm so glad to see both of you. I really wanted to talk to you.'

'About what?' asked Aditya.

'We're planning a trip to Malaysia this year. You must give me some travel tips.'

'Ask Prachi. She's the authority on the subject.' Aditya quickly washed his hands of the matter.

'I will.' Smita turned to Prachi, 'Can we talk now?'

'Sure.'

'Come, let's sit somewhere.'

Before she could walk away, Aditya stopped Smita with a question.

'How are things with you?'

Smita knew what Aditya was trying to find out, but like always, she preferred to deflect the question with banalities.

'It's all good. We went on a holiday last week to the Jog Falls, but it was a short trip. So we are planning to take a long vacation in Malaysia and Singapore around the New Year. I'm really looking forward to the shopping.'

Aditya decided to be direct.

'How's your father, Smita?'

There was a short silence. She replied carefully.

'Everything has been taken care of. Baba is doing extremely well; none of the crazy talk and no imaginary problems.'

'He wasn't crazy. He had a serious delusionary problem and it needed immediate attention. He...'

'It has been done,' she butted in sunnily.

Aditya was relieved, 'So he visited a psychiatrist?'

'No, not really. It turns out that it wasn't a psychiatric problem at all. To tell you the truth, I had my doubts from the beginning. There's an old man in my father's department who spends all his time in Shakti *puja*. When my father was given an award sometime back, this man became jealous and did something to Baba's mind. My mother contacted a famous priest from the Shani temple who can undo the effects of black magic. He did a Shani *puja* followed by a *homa* and Baba is absolutely normal now.'

Aditya couldn't believe his ears. How could an educated person like her talk about black magic and priestly interventions?

'I'm not sure that's the right approach,' he said. 'Nihilistic delusion can be very dangerous.'

Smita snapped at him:

'I'm telling you that Baba did not have nihilistic delusion – it was a clear case of jealousy and resentment. He's fine now and his illness is a closed chapter. Come, Prachi, let's sit on the couches there.'

Aditya watched the two women settle down on one of the sofas. He felt uneasy throughout the evening.

***

The unease continued for days after that and Aditya had no idea why. He tried to cope with the feeling, but found it increasingly difficult to remain optimistic that entire festive season. Maybe it was the weather, he thought. Bangalore was having unseasonal torrents of rain and as a result, there were frequent power cuts, the city roads were water logged and the traffic was messy.

Thankfully, the weather changed over the weekend and it stopped raining. But it was a short respite. When he drove to the clinic the following Monday, it seemed like it was going to pour again.

A few patients turned up without appointments and they needed to be accommodated. His day was long and tiring. Finally, Aditya had some time to himself after dinner. Just as he started reading a book in bed, the phone rang. It was Mrs Nayak, mother of one of his patients. She constantly called him on his cell phone despite his telling her that it was only for emergencies.

Mrs Nayak's daughter was Ishita – a young girl in her twenties who was once treated for bipolar disorder and had responded well to the treatment. She had found a good job and was now married to her college sweetheart. But her mother remained apprehensive. Aditya sympathised with her – the anxiety about a child who had severe bouts of bipolarity could not simply be wiped away, but she should not call him at odd hours for non-emergencies.

Many times, Aditya seriously considered blocking the number. He let the phone ring.

Prachi was lying next to him on the bed and got annoyed.

'Why don't you answer the call? If you don't want to talk, switch off the phone. I'm trying to sleep.'

Aditya was peeved. He could not do what he wanted even in his own house. He pressed the talk button on his phone and said curtly, 'Yes, Mrs Nayak?'

Ishita's mother sensed his brusque manner and said apologetically:

'Hello, Doctor. I hope I didn't wake you up.'

'No, I was reading a book.' He softened his voice, 'How is Ishita?'

'All okay, I think.'

Then she shouldn't have called him at this time. He looked at the wall clock. It was 9:45. He tried to be as polite as possible and asked:

'Why did you call?'

'I wanted to talk to you. Ishita and her husband have relocated to Chandigarh. I think I told you about it when I spoke with you on our last call.'

'Yes,' he replied in monosyllabically.

'I think Chandigarh is not working out for her. I sense some inconsistencies.'

'Is Ishita taking her medicines regularly?'

'Yes, she is… I think she is.'

'Then that should work for now. But if you have any concerns, then advise her to go to a local psychiatrist.' There was nothing more he could do without seeing the patient.

'That's why I called you. Do you know any one there, Doctor? I am planning to go to Chandigarh in a few days and I can take her to the psychiatrist during my visit.'

'I'm sorry, I don't know anyone in Chandigarh, but Ishita can always take a referral from a friend or a colleague.'

Mrs Nayak hesitated.

'If she asks around, then everyone will know about her condition. You know how fast this sort of news travels. We must be discreet about it.'

'Mrs Nayak, anyone can have a disorder. What's there to hide? But if you still feel that way, I suggest you talk to a general physician in Chandigarh, get a reference from him and take Ishita to a psychiatrist. She is much better now and you must take care that she doesn't go back to where she was years ago.'

'I'll try. Thanks, Doctor. Goodnight.'

As he put the phone down, Prachi asked:

'Who was that?'

'Rama Nayak. She's the mother of one of my patients.'

'Why did she call at this hour? Is there a problem?'

Aditya shook his head.

'Not really. She wanted the contact details of a psychiatrist in Chandigarh.'

'So why didn't you give it to her?'

'Must I know psychiatrists from every part of the world?'

'Maybe you don't know anyone in Chandigarh, but someone in your network would know, correct?' Prachi insisted. 'Mrs Nayak must have called you with such a lot of expectation and look at you – you washed your hands of her without even trying.'

'How much is enough? There's no end to the long list of patients' never-ending problems,' said Aditya. He was getting more irritated.

'So? You are a doctor. Isn't it your duty to help them?' Prachi questioned him and turned away to face the wall. She stayed that way the entire night.

On Tuesday morning, the rains stopped, but the skies were dark and the world continued to look grim. Prachi stayed aloof from her husband. Aditya tried to appease her, but she ignored him. When he asked her to join him for breakfast, she looked away.

'I will eat later. You go ahead,' she said sullenly.

He showered and ate his breakfast alone.

'When will you eat, Prachi? It's almost eight. Don't you have to go to the hospital?' he asked her gently, before leaving for his clinic.

'I don't feel like…'

'Are you annoyed with me because I was curt with Mrs Nayak last night?'

'No.'

'Okay, I'll find a good psychiatrist in Chandigarh from my friends in Delhi and I'll give Mrs Nayak all the details.'

'Fine.'

'Now smile.'

She didn't smile nor did she reply.

Aditya tried again.

'Have I done something wrong? Did I say something to hurt you?'

'No. Nothing.'

'Are you feeling alright?'

'Why wouldn't I?'

Aditya was at the end of his patience. Why were women so difficult? He decided to leave before the conversation escalated into an argument.

'I'm leaving Prachi. I'll see you later, okay? Bye.'

She did not even look at him.

22

'How many appointments do I have today?' Aditya paused at Aruna's desk.

'None in the afternoon, Sir. There were three appointments in the morning, but one of the patients, Tanushree Mallick, called a few minutes ago and cancelled today's session.'

This was the third time Tanushree had cancelled her appointment. Aditya hoped that she wasn't getting lax in her treatment. He made a mental note to send her an email. Thankfully, she was very prompt in replying to emails.

'So, two appointments in the morning. Anybody new?' he asked. The first session with a patient was always demanding and he did not have the energy for it today.

'No, the first appointment is with Sunita and the next one is with Kabir.'

When Aditya had first met Sunita four years ago, she was an acute bulimia patient. Though she'd had very few relapses since then and was on the road to recovery, he continued to closely monitor her. A few more sessions and then Sunita would need to come in only for quarterly checkups.

Kabir's case also had a simple diagnosis. The man was suffering from depression and a regular low-dosage anti-depressant would hopefully solve the problem. Aditya needed to see his blood reports before prescribing the medicine.

Good, he thought, now that there were just two patients to see, he could go home early today and relax.

'I have a headache, Aruna. Can you please get me some aspirin?' he said.

She was concerned.

'Sure. I'll bring it to your room right now. Would you like some coffee, Sir?'

'No, the caffeine may aggravate it. Would you make me a cup of green tea instead?'

'Of course,' she replied and walked into the small kitchenette.

Aditya went into his room and switched on the laptop. He hadn't checked his email for over fourteen hours now. Unfortunately, the Internet connection today was inordinately slow. When the browser finally opened, he was surprised to see thirty-one new emails in his inbox. Most of the mails were junk; he deleted the chain mails, emails from pharmaceutical companies and forwards from acquaintances.

But there was the email from Psychiatric Research Society. Aditya clicked on the mail. Nothing happened. He clicked again and found himself offline. The network was down. He was exasperated with everything.

'Aruna, have you switched off the modem?' he asked loudly. When Aruna was new to the clinic, she sometimes used to do that.

'No, Sir, but the Internet has been slow all morning. I have already complained to the service provider and they have promised to send someone by lunchtime.'

Aditya was not going to wait till lunch to read the response from the Psychiatric Research Society. After all, he also needed to prepare for his presentation and make plans for the conference at Perth. There was no time to waste or wait. He rebooted his computer, but it didn't help. Then he switched off the modem and waited for three seconds before switching it back on.

This time, it worked.

Quickly, he opened the email only to realise that the news wasn't good. The Society had rejected his paper. The short email from the panel coordinator said that the subject had promise, but the research results were too preliminary to be presented in the upcoming conference. She suggested that Aditya resubmit the paper the next year with more substantive evidence. Of course, he was invited to attend the conference, though he'd have to take care of the logistics and expenses himself.

Aditya shut down the computer and tried to calm his mind. Sunita was expected at any moment and he could not afford to stay disgruntled and unhappy. He had the morning to get through.

***

After the appointment with Kabir, Aditya was packing his brown leather bag and about to leave for the day when he heard Aruna talking to someone in the reception area.

A minute later, the door opened. Aruna looked flustered as she said, 'Sir, Mrs Shabnam wants to meet you.'

'Who?'

'Shabnam. Dr Jonathan Das had sent her to us and she had brought in her husband Ali months ago.'

Aditya was surprised.

'Yes, yes, I remember her. Was she supposed to come in today?'

'No. She doesn't have an appointment, but she's so upset that…'

'It's okay, Aruna. Send her in.'

Shabnam walked into the room and sat down with her eyes downcast. She looked dishevelled, gaunt and fatigued.

'Is everything okay, Shabnam?' Aditya was concerned at her appearance.

She started sobbing.

'What happened?'

'My husband… he's in jail.'

Oh God. Aditya was shocked.

'Why? What did he do?'

'He is in jail,' she repeated.

'Did he…?'

Shabnam nodded.

'Yes… This time my son's in-laws were at home… Things became ugly and my husband picked up an iron rod and hit my son's father-in-law on the head. He may not… may not make it.'

She gulped. 'I have managed to find a lawyer. He says that if you give a report saying that my husband has a mental disorder, then the judge might be a little lenient with him.'

'But, Shabnam, your husband never came back for a second visit. I didn't get a chance to treat him...'

'But you knew that he was unwell.' She looked at him pleadingly. 'You told me.'

'Yes, I did. But I didn't come to a proper diagnosis, because he didn't take the tests I suggested.'

She was desperate and insisted, 'That doesn't matter. Please write what you suspected. I'm sure that it will count.'

Aditya doubted it very much. He told her he would think it over, that she should check with him the next day. Shabnam went back with a hope that he would give her a certificate.

Aditya felt mentally drained. He clutched his head with both his hands. The double aspirins should have worked by now. He wished he could get a respite from work for a few days.

Frustrated, Aditya picked up his bag and marched out of the office, leaving Aruna in charge for the rest of the day.

As he started the car, Aditya wondered about the situation at home. Prachi had been in such a gloomy mood in the morning and he sincerely hoped that she was now over it.

Back at home, he noticed his wife's car in the garage. Why hadn't she gone to the hospital today?

'What happened?' He asked her with concern. 'How come you didn't go to the hospital today? Are you okay?'

Prachi came over and hugged him.

'Sorry. Yesterday was a tough day at work and I was feeling crappy. I didn't mean to snap at you.'

'It's okay, Prachi.' Aditya held her tightly.

'I decided to take the day off. My colleague said that he will take care of the appointments.'

'Good.'

'I was about to have lunch. Come, let us eat. After that I would like to take some more rest.'

'Me too. I have a headache.'

'Oh.'

Prachi walked into the kitchen.

Aditya wished that his wife would have fussed a little more about his headache, but then she was also stressed out. It wasn't the right time to grumble about her inattentiveness. Wasn't she the first to hug?

Aditya had his lunch and stretched out on the bed next to Prachi.

When he woke up an hour later, the headache was gone. Thank God for that. Aditya got up, made some tea and sat down in his study. But he just could not concentrate. He tried again after dinner. But he continued to feel restless. Finally, he came back to the bedroom where Prachi was reading a book in bed.

He sat next to his wife.

'I got a mail from the Psychiatric Research Society today. They've rejected my paper,' he said.

'What?' She put the book aside and looked disappointed. 'I was really looking forward to Australia.'

Aditya could not believe it. She was disappointed about a cancelled trip to Australia, but what about his paper? He had pinned all his hopes on it for months on end, only to be rejected. Didn't she care?

He let it go.

'Shall we go and sit in the garden for a while?'

'No, I want to finish this book. It's very interesting,' she said and went back to reading.

'Okay.'

Aditya went to the living room and turned on the television. He channel-surfed. After looking at the local news, which was preoccupied with the weather, some sports and other inane stuff, he settled on a rerun of a James Bond movie on HBO.

23

A burst of thunder woke him up. He realised that he had dozed off while watching television. Sleepily, he peered at his watch; it was ten at night.

Just then, his phone started to ring. He groaned when he saw that the call was from an unknown number. It must be a patient like Mrs Nayak with a trivial question. For a second, he was irritated, but then it might be someone with a real emergency. He picked up the phone.

The connection was terrible and there was a lot of static, but there was no doubt who the caller was – it was Prakash. At last!

'It's time you called. Where have you been all these days? You never bothered to send me your contact details,' Aditya complained.

'I'm so sorry! I was trying to get settled here in Cape Town and time just flew by. Have you heard from Deepa?'

Aditya was surprised at the sudden and abrupt change of subject. Besides, that should have been his question to Prakash. He said, 'In fact, I wanted to talk to you about her.'

'Oh! So you've heard from her recently?'

'No, no, I haven't heard from her in months. That's why I wanted to speak with you. My last contact with her was almost twenty months back. She was going to let me know her wedding date, but I never received any information. I also became busy after that and could not keep in touch. I tried to send her an email in August, but it bounced back. I was wondering whether she has changed her email id…' Aditya's voice trailed off.

After a few seconds of silence, Prakash replied.

'Deepa's wedding never happened. In fact, she's no longer in London. She's in Jaipur.'

'Jaipur? Why?'

'I wish I knew. I was pre-occupied with settling down in a new country. I had to find a house, get school admissions and figure out my new responsibilities at work. A few days back, when I phoned Deepa's father, he told me that she had moved to Jaipur and that he was going to relocate too. When I asked him what had happened, he said he was not sure and gave me her number. I called her, but she was evasive. All I gathered was that it had something to do with Raj. Since you were Raj's doctor before she left for London, I thought that she might have got in touch with you.'

'No, she didn't. Give me her number. I'll try and talk to her.'

'The phone number is…'

Aditya snatched a piece of paper and noted it down.

'Let me know what you find. Meanwhile, I will send my contact details by email.'

'Okay. Bye, Prakash.'

It was too late to phone Deepa, Aditya told himself, as he walked to the bedroom. He would wait till tomorrow. He stretched out on the bed, but sleep eluded him. Myriad thoughts continued to bother him and it was only hours later that he fell into a fitful sleep.

The alarm went off in the morning, but Aditya slept through it. The cleaning woman rang the bell a little later, but he did not stir. The mechanical humming of the air-conditioner only further lulled him to sleep.

Finally, Prachi nudged him, 'Wake up. It's late and you may not reach your clinic on time.'

Aditya groaned. He didn't want to wake up; he just wanted to be left alone.

But Prachi refused to give up. She switched off the air conditioner and pulled back the curtains.

***

'How is your headache, Sir?' Aruna asked when she saw Aditya enter the clinic.

'I am okay. By the way, I have an important phone call to make. Send the first patient after that, please.'

'Sure, Sir.'

Aditya walked into his room and dialled Deepa's number. Her cell phone was unreachable. He waited for five minutes and tried again with the same result. He hoped the number Prakash had given him was correct.

His morning went off as usual. After the last patient left, Aditya looked out of the window. It seemed the weatherman's prediction was finally coming true. It was raining and the trees on both sides of the road were swaying to mild gusts of wind. Then he remembered Deepa. Her phone was probably still unreachable, but he would try one more time. He punched in the number. The phone started ringing. Thank God.

'Hello?'

'Deepa?'

There was a pause.

'Aditya! Did Prakash give you my number to spy on me?' She sounded bitter.

He did not take offence.

'Yes, Prakash gave me your number. He said that you are in Jaipur now. When did you move?'

'Around five months ago, though it feels more like five decades.'

'What are you doing there?' he asked softly.

'Trying to stay alive.'

'Why did you leave London?' he probed.

'Don't ask me questions that have no easy answers.'

'I know that life has been very rough on you, Deepa, but you must–'

'Oh, please stop preaching! It's easy for a psychiatrist to give advice. Do you really understand what people like me go through?' She took a deep breath and tried to control herself. She wasn't talking to just any psychiatrist; this was Aditya – a friend and a genuine well-wisher.

'I'm sorry,' she said. 'I'm trying to be strong and take charge of my life. Had I given up trying, then I would have probably jumped in front of a running train by now.'

Aditya was alarmed.

'Deepa, what's going on? How's Raj?'

'Hanging in there, I guess.'

'Please, tell me what happened.'

'Raj became really sick… Someone told me about Jaipur and I came here.' She was still vague.

'Tell me everything properly, Deepa. You had written to me that Raj was happy in London. What changed?'

'There's no point in discussing the past…'

Aditya interrupted her.

'I want to know. I was Raj's first psychiatrist and he had responded well to my treatment.'

'Yes, he had. Maybe I should have stayed back here in India and not pursued my own happiness.'

'Does this have something to do with Ethan?'

'Who?' Deepa sounded confused for a moment. Then she said, 'No, it has nothing to do with him.'

He waited for her to elaborate.

'Aditya, I have to go now. I'm in the office and shouldn't be taking personal calls during business hours.'

'Will you call me in the evening, then?'

'I'll try.'

'I'll wait for your call.'

Deepa hung up without bothering to say goodbye.

*****

Aditya wondered if she would really call back. She did. She phoned him around nine, soon after dinner as he was putting the leftovers in the fridge. Prachi was in bed, back to the book that she was reading.

'I thought you forgot.' Aditya pulled out a dining chair and sat down.

'I got late in the office today.' She sounded tired.

He did not waste any time and quickly came to the point.

'We were discussing Raj in the afternoon. What changed?'

'It was all very gradual and the changes were so minor that they escaped me. I'm such a fool – a big fool. After Raj adjusted well to his new psychiatrist and therapist, I was relieved and started making plans for the wedding. I assumed that Raj had become normal and when he asked me to give him some independence, I let him take charge.'

'Didn't he take his medicines regularly?'

'No, he lied to me. One day, I discovered that Raj was not his usual self. Something about his behaviour bothered me. So I questioned him. I found out that he had a girlfriend. Can you imagine? Him having a girlfriend?'

That wasn't relevant to the topic of discussion at all. Deepa had decided to raise her son in London, but was annoyed that he had found a girlfriend? It didn't make any sense.

'Why not?'

'Aditya, there would have been no problem had she been a regular girl. In fact, I would have been happy.'

'What do you mean "regular girl"?'

'Do you remember Bobby?'

'Of course, I remember him. He was Raj's imaginary friend...' Aditya stopped.

'Yes, just like Bobby was Raj's best friend, this imaginary Rebecca became his girlfriend. It was a nightmare. She was always with Raj and then the violence started again. He blamed her for everything. At first, the ruckus began at home and then it moved to the neighbourhood. One day, Raj broke into a neighbour's house, who immediately called me. Do you know what reason Raj gave? He said that the neighbour had locked up Rebecca and the voices had told him to go save her.'

'Voices?'

'Yes, it was then that I learnt about him hearing voices again.' Deepa stopped for a moment and continued, 'Ethan and I took Raj to his psychiatrist right away. He said that Raj had not taken the medicines for a long time and his schizophrenia was full blown.'

Aditya nodded to himself. Raj was in a psychotic crisis and imprisoned in an unreal world where voices guided him and told him to do things. Just like his father. He could be subdued by strong medicines, but a return to normal was completely out of the question.

Deepa's only option was to put Raj in an institution where trained people could handle him. Ethan located such an institution an hour away from

London, but it was very expensive and she wouldn't have been able to afford it on a long-term basis. Ethan was willing to take the responsibility – financial and otherwise, but Deepa couldn't let him do it. Over time, she broke up with Ethan, knowing very well that he would be upset for a while, but that he would move on eventually. She felt horrible for spilling over her endless problems on someone else.

'So you left London and came to Jaipur?'

'Yes, a friend recommended a place in Jaipur. Though it's supposed to be an institution, it's really a rented house turned into a home for about fifteen chronic schizophrenia patients. The owner's son has schizophrenia and he keeps him there too. It is a decent place with round-the-clock nursing care.'

'A good place like that must not be cheap.'

'It isn't, but it is still much cheaper than such places in London. I sold my house along with everything and put the money in a fixed deposit. That money should be enough to take care of Raj as long as he lives.' Her voice broke.

'And what about you?'

'What about me? I manage. I have found work in a company. The salary is not much. I have a two-room flat, but it's okay. My father refuses to leave me alone. He wants to sell the Bangalore house, move here to Jaipur and buy a place.' Her voice dropped. 'So that's how things are.'

Aditya was not ready to let her go.

'Can you send me your journal?' he asked.

'My what?' Deepa was puzzled.

'You know, your journal – where you write down things and your reactions. Maybe there's something in there… a clue perhaps, that would give me a lead and help me find a line of treatment for Raj. There are new studies and new theories coming up all the time; maybe there's a way around.'

'Are all psychiatrists so optimistic? Or are you an exception, Aditya?' Deepa said. 'There's no journal anymore. I stopped writing a while ago.'

'Okay. But I want to talk to you about Raj. I need to know more.' He didn't want to give up. There must be something he could do.

'I really don't know how it's going to be useful. But if you insist, I can meet you when I come to Bangalore.'

'When will that be?'

'I don't know. Maybe next month, or the month after that.' She sounded weary. 'Tomorrow is another long and tough day. I must get some rest.'

After hanging up, Aditya sat at the dining table for a long time, staring at the blank wall in front of him. A lizard on the wall was stalking a moth, but he didn't notice it. The rain and the wind had calmed down outside the window, but a tempest raged inside him.

***

It was well past midnight when Aditya crawled into bed and fell into a deep slumber. The alarm on his cell phone went off as usual at six. He turned it off and tried to go back to sleep. He was about to doze off again when Prachi nudged him.

'Aditya, get ready quickly. We have to go,' she said with great urgency in her voice.

'Go where?' He opened his eyes groggily.

'Jayant called. He was trying you, but your phone was probably on silent. It is about his father-in-law.'

'Why? What happened? Another occurrence of nihilistic delusion?' Aditya yawned.

'Smita's father died last night.'

'What?' Aditya sat up.

'He went to bed early. His wife was watching TV in the living room. She went into their bedroom sometime after midnight and switched on the light. She found her husband dead. There was blood everywhere. He had slashed his wrists with a kitchen knife. Jayant said that Smita is in bad shape. She is absolutely inconsolable.'

Aditya was dazed. One more failure. Another sad ending.

At some level, was it his fault? Should he have been more forceful in insisting that the family take Smita's father to a psychiatrist? All the cases with sad endings filled up his thoughts. There was Raj and then there was Shabnam's husband Ali…

At that moment, Aditya suddenly felt useless.

***

Over the next few days, Prachi noticed her husband's melancholy; he was brooding a lot but she left him alone to give him some space. A psychiatrist's job wasn't easy. The balance was always tilted – there were just too many disappointments.

However, soon she realised that there was something more, something deeper, bothering her husband; it wasn't mere disappointment. She couldn't remain a silent spectator any more.

One night as they were winding down in bed, Prachi prodded him gently into a conversation about life and work. What started as half-sentences soon turned into a serious conversation. In its course, she found out that Aditya was being very hard on himself.

Prachi wondered how she could cheer her husband up. Maybe she should bring up all the positive cases that he had shared with her. There were Sunita, Jonathan, Tanushree and so many other people. If she discussed them, maybe Aditya would see his efforts had not been useless. That he had done a great job as a psychiatrist. She also realised that Aditya was constantly keeping a huge burden all to himself. Prachi moved a little closer to Aditya.

'You know, Aditya, I feel you should take the plunge now and build an organisation.'

Aditya reacted the same way that he always did.

'I don't think that I have what it takes.'

'Of course you do.' Her voice was quite insistent this time. 'I'm not asking you to take the entire responsibility upon yourself. Talk to a few psychiatrist friends and find out what they think.

You could first reach out to Jonathan, who's already interested and maybe you can talk to Anjana for the therapy side of things. If they feel the way you do, then just think how much you could help people with a multi-disciplinary mental health hospital at your disposal. You could have a helpline, then expand progressively, add a few beds for emergency cases.'

Aditya was quiet in a contemplative way.

She touched his hand smiled and added, 'And if you'll take me, I can be with you part-time and help with some of the stuff.'

He looked at her and pulled her close to him. They stayed that way for a long time. Prachi fell asleep, but Aditya was awake for hours that night.

Aditya's intercom buzzed.

'Yes, Aruna?'

'Sir, your next patient is here. May I send her in?'

'Sure.'

Tanushree walked into Aditya's room looking pretty in a purple silk sari.

'Hello, Doctor, what a lovely day outside.' There was sunshine in her voice.

Aditya smiled.

'Hi, Tanushree. How are you?'

'I'm fine, Doctor. How are things with you?'

'All okay. But I haven't seen you in a while. Weren't you supposed to be here last month? Aruna said you cancelled your appointment.'

'Yes, Doctor, I'm so sorry.' She looked sheepish. 'But you know what, I have been promoted recently. I am now the Chief Marketing Officer of the company.'

'Congratulations! That's really nice!'

'Thank you. In my new role, I have to travel much more frequently. Sometimes at short notice. That's why I had to cancel my appointments with you. But look, here I am today.'

'I hope you are taking your medicines regularly and your travel has not disrupted your routine.'

'Of course not! I'm very diligent with the meds and also with my therapy; I've never missed a single one of those till now. Oh yes, I did get the blood work done. I had asked the lab to send the results to you directly. Have you seen the reports?'

'I did. Everything's normal.' He skimmed through the report one more time.

'Thank God. But I think you may have to reassess the medicine that I'm taking in the mornings. They make me a little drowsy.'

Aditya looked up her last prescription and just as he was about to write a change, Tanushree said, 'I have something for you, Doctor.' She opened her bag and took out a small package wrapped in aluminium foil.

'What's that?' asked Aditya as she unwrapped it.

'Chocolate cake.'

'Where did you get that from?'

'It's homemade.'

'Well then, who baked it?'

She smiled mysteriously. 'Take a guess.'

'Your mother-in-law?'

Tanushree broke into peals of laughter.

'Doctor, must you tease me? I was the one in the kitchen all morning; I did all the work.'

Aditya smiled and picked up a piece of the cake.

***

As Tanushree left after her session, Aditya impulsively opened his laptop and wrote an email to Jonathan.

Dear Jonathan,

I have been thinking about something for a long time and today I must share it with you.

I feel I am now ready to take the plunge. I will speak to Anjana as well. Let's get together and discuss the future. Could we all meet at my place this weekend? Prachi has been after me to take the next big leap, just as you have. Maybe the reason and season are now here.

Jonathan, I've always admired you for your commitment to the cause of mental health. Perhaps we could work together. Do give me a call when you are free.

Warm regards,

Aditya

As he hit the send button, a wonderful sense of optimism engulfed him. He picked up the phone and called Prachi.

www.ingramcontent.com/pod-product-compliance
Lightning Source LLC
Chambersburg PA
CBHW021142260726
48656CB00024B/1180